The Top of Whitley

- a study of the Spring Gardens area of Reading, Berkshire, England

by

Daphne Joyce Barnes-Phillips, MA (Ed), BA (Hons)

"A city built on a hill cannot be hidden" - Matthew 5 v. 14

Copyright details

Published by: Corridor Press
Midleton House
5 Erleigh Road
Reading
Berkshire
RG1 5LR
England
Tel: (0118) 9872017
E-mail: springgardens@yahoo.co.uk
Website: http://www.readingchurches.org.uk/Whitley

Printed and bound in Great Britain by: Antony Rowe Ltd
Bumper's Farm
Chippenham
Wiltshire
SN14 6LH
Tel: (01249) 659705
E-mail: 100616.40@compuserve.com
Website: http://www.antonyrowe.co.uk

ISBN: 1 – 897715 – 01 – 3

Spring Gardens

Publications

Acknowledgements

As well as those who are mentioned in the Sources section at the back of this book for having shared their memories with me, either by writing them down or telling me them orally, I should like to thank the following:

Len Cook who produced most of the sketches used, including that of the original Whitley Pump for the front cover and page 150;

Those who lent or gave photographs, Minutes Books and other items;

Berkshire Record Office and the Local Studies section of Reading Central Library;

My husband, Jim Barnes-Phillips, for encouraging me to finally publish "The Top of Whitley", taking the modern day photographs and doing much of the donkey work in scanning in the older photographs and sketches;

Members of Corridor Press, Reading, Berkshire, who continued that encouragement, especially Ron Pearce who proof-read and Alison Haymonds who gave me hints as to how to proceed;

Finally, those who have waited so patiently for this record to be completed.

Dedication

This book is dedicated to the memory of my much-loved parents:

ROSE ALICE BARNES who first introduced me to Whitley Hall Methodist Church Sunday School

Rose is pictured here (centre of back row) as Leader of the 1st Reading Girls' Brigade Explorers in 1969 in Whitley Hall's Small Schoolroom with the 5-7 year old girls and helpers (from left: Ruth Bainton, Theresa Saunders, Pamela Bainton and Joyce Woodcraft). As part of their Collectors badge, the Explorers had been collecting milk tops towards the purchase of a guide dog.

and ALBERT EDWARD BARNES who was himself, at one time, a member of that same Sunday School

Ted is pictured here with the last sackfulls of milktops needed to purchase Guide Dog "TOPSIE" in 1972 after Rose's death. Behind him is one of the sheds he constructed especially to store the milktops.

- and to all those connected with WHITLEY HALL METHODIST CHURCH who have befriended and influenced me throughout my life.

The Top of Whitley

- a study of the Spring Gardens area of Reading

Intro - The Source: How the topic came to be chosen Page 9

I. Springing Up: Description of the growth of the Spring Gardens area after the construction of Reading's second reservoir there in 1818; including the Conduit Close controversy and burglaries in 1833 Page 13

II. The First Trickle: The first inhabitants who, by 1842 included 6 with the Christian name John, 4 James and 4 Thomas out of 16 occupiers! The sale by auction of land under the will of John Boult who died in 1848 Page 21

III. On Tap: 4 beer shops out of 19 inhabited dwellings in 1842! but then beer was part of the staple diet in the 1830s at St Giles' Workhouse when each man was allowed 21 pints of beer a week and each woman or child 10 pints. Wellington Arms, Whitley Street is the sole survivor today Page 29

IV. Opening the Flood Gates: the population grew; services were held from 1840 and a Wesleyan Methodist Chapel was started before 1853, then extended from one cottage to take over two prior to 1870, when the foundation stone of a purpose-built Chapel, Spring Gardens Mission, was laid on Wednesday, August 31st Page 35

V. Educating the Off-Spring: Spring Gardens Sunday School (1856) which transferred to new premises when Whitley Hall Mission was built in 1906; and Christ Church School (1868) Page 47

VI. And the Banned Played On: Formed between 1884 - 93, Spring Gardens Mission Prize Band was prevented from playing in a Public Park in 1909 and for the 21st Anniversary of the Trades Union Congress in 1912. It eventually separated from Whitley Hall Methodist Church in 1934 and is still playing today as Spring Gardens Band Page 59

VII. Let Us Play: Recreational activities in Spring Gardens were based at the Church (especially Choir and Women's Own); Christ Church Institute and the Tank, after it became a Pleasure Ground in 1902 Page 65

VIII. Full To The Brim: Opening Ceremony of Whitley Hall in 1906 Page 77

IX. Still Waters Run Deep: Spring Gardens area after Whitley Hall was built Page 89

X. The Tributaries: PSA, Band of Hope, Slate Clubs, Boys' and Girls' Brigades and Wesley Guild were some of the activities available Page 97

XI. Bridge Over Troubled Waters: How the two World Wars affected life, both during them (1914 - 18 and 1939 - 45) and afterwards Page 109

XII. Flushed With Success: Whitley Hall's Sunday School became the largest in Reading in 1934 with 496 scholars and 57 teachers Page 121

XIII. Mortlake: The Spring Gardens area was compulsorily purchased, demolished and rebuilt in the 1960s - 1970s. The Wilkins family from Whitley Street took part in the BBC documentary 'The Family' (1974) and the interior of Pottinger's Barber Shop was reconstructed in Blake's Lock Museum (1984) Page 137

XIV. Digging New Channels: Spring Gardens area in recent years, including the Reading Borough Link Scheme with the Church, the arrival of the Seventh Day Adventist Church, the sale of the Whitley Hall premises and the reopening of New Christ Church CE (Voluntary Aided) Primary under the Government's Fresh Start initiative Page 141

List of **Lay Pastors and Ministers** who served Whitley Hall Mission and Methodist Church, their dates of service and the main events that occurred during their ministry in the Spring Gardens area and also in the Reading Circuit, which is now known as the Reading and Silchester Circuit Page 151

List of **Sources** Page 154

List of Illustrations

List of Illustrations	Page
1st Reading Girls' Brigade Explorers with sacks of milktops in 1969	4
Ted Barnes with sacks of milktops collected for guide dog "Topsie" in 1972	5
Presentation of Photograph of Guide Dog "Rose", 1977	10
Sketch of the spring in Conduit Close	15
Conduit Crescent with replica Whitley Pump, May 2000	16
Whitley Hall Choir Outing by wagonette – early 1920s	20
Plan of the Parish of St Giles in 1840	22
1899 Map of Spring Gardens area	28
The Wellington Arms in modern day Whitley Street, January 2001	34
Spring Gardens Mission Hall, Lynn Street. (Sketch by Len Cook)	38
Dedication plate in Sunday School attendance prize, 1894	49
Rev W Beddard Smith helping renovate Whitley Hall in 1950	50
New Christ Church C of E Primary School, Spring Gardens in January 2001	58
Spring Gardens Wesleyan Mission Band, 1902	63
Starisers Drum & Bugle Corp leading Whitley Hall's Sunday School, 1986	64
Memories of "Football in the Tank". (Sketch by Len Cook)	66
Whitley Hall Football Club, 1923/4 – Championship winning team	69
Whitley Hall Harvest Festival, 1920 with Pastor Bert Bailey	70
Whitley Hall Choir with Rev Noel Richardson	72
1849 Auction particulars of land on which Whitley Hall was built	23 & 78
Dedication of Children's Corner with Rev E Donald Mason, 1973	80
Sketch of Whitley Hall at time of opening in March 1906	82
Wednesday afternoon Wedding outside Whitley Hall, July 1953	83
Opening of Whitley Hall on 14th March, 1906	88
Photograph of the original Whitley Pump	92
Photograph of modern day replica of Whitley Pump, 2000	94
Eldorado icecream salesman on tricycle	95
Rainbow Bazaar Programme, January/February 1928	102
"Farley Goes Out" with Pastor Spargo, January 1930	107
Certificate of Appreciation to Pastor Bert Bailey, August 1922	110
Nativity Tableau from "Living Statuary", November 1948	117
Rev Wilfred White meeting the President of Conference, Bristol 1948	120
Missionary Play produced by Sunday School including Len Rapley	122
AREFF's cartoon of Sunday School outing to Leighton Park grounds	125
Sunday School Concert in Whitley Hall Church, 1921	126
Presentation of MYED Long Service Certificates to Sunday School Staff	133
Rose Barnes and 1st Reading Explorers counting halfpennies, 1968	134
Nativity Scene from Sunday School Toy Service, December 1986	136
Map of Spring Gardens area of Reading in 1990s	143
Lord Soper's visit to Reading for 250th anniversary celebrations, 1988	153

Introduction: The Source

I heard the voice of Jesus say:
'Behold, I freely give
The living water; thirsty one,
Stoop down and drink and live'.
I came to Jesus, and I drank
Of that live-giving stream;
My thirst was quenched, my soul revived,
And now I live in Him.

Verse 2 of no 136 in Hymns & Psalms
by Horatius Bonar (1808 - 1889)

The idea for this book sprang from my work as superintendent of Whitley Hall Sunday School, to which I was promoted in 1984 after 22 years' service.

During 1986, when the Sunday School, as well as Whitley Hall Methodist Church, was celebrating its 80th Anniversary in its present building, I wanted the then Sunday School members to be able to appreciate some of the tremendous heritage that was their's. Two former Sunday School members who had become ministers of religion (and one a missionary as well) led worship on the anniversary day. I also asked for others who, like myself, had been brought up in Whitley Hall Sunday School to assist them by choosing hymns, doing Bible readings, leading prayers, acting as organists, church and door stewards and arranging flowers for the morning and evening services.

While talking to those who had been members of the Sunday School in its early years at Whitley Hall, I discovered that they all still enthused about the annual Sunday School treat. As a result, I was able to instigate the re-enactment of one of those to Leighton Park School grounds during the anniversary afternoon. Past and present members marched there behind our own Starisers Drum and Bugle Corps but listened to the Spring Gardens Band, which had had connections with Whitley Hall's predecessor (Spring Gardens Mission) and with Whitley Hall itself until 1934, when we arrived at Leighton Park. We had races as well but returned to Whitley Hall for the tea and evening service rather than stay there into the evening as our forefathers had done when the event was held mid-week.

While making plans for that special anniversary, various people supplied me with their photographs and reminiscences. As well as using some of those on the day, I also reproduced others in our church magazine, *Newslink*, of which I was an editor. This started a regular feature which continued until the magazine ceased production at the end of 1997. It also meant that I was loaned the *minutes books* of various activities connected with both Whitley Hall and its predecessor, Spring Gardens Mission, and so an interest in writing a history of the two churches developed.

The above photograph, taken by the Reading Chronicle, had been used on the front cover of the Girls' Brigade magazine and, even more interestingly, on the back page of the 1977 Royal Albert Hall Programme for the Girls' Brigade Display with Her Majesty Queen Elizabeth II in her Jubilee Year on the front page. It shows Beatrice Silk presenting the 1st Reading Explorers with a photograph of Guide Dog "Rose".

Having been introduced to Whitley Hall's Sunday School as a three-year-old by my mother, Rose Barnes, I was to remain associated with it, and the church, for half a century. Obviously, during that time, as well as being made a member of the Church, along with eight others, on 11th February, 1962, I have been a member of many of the church's other activities, including Girls' Life Brigade, Junior Christian Endeavour, Youth Club and the Harmony Gospel Group. In August 1980, Jim and I married at Whitley Hall and I became its Senior Church Steward from May 1986 until April 1988 then again from May 1996 until the sale of the building in December 1997, during two six year periods as a Church Steward. Throughout those times, I represented it at Reading and Silchester Circuit level and have also represented the Circuit at the Southampton District Synod of the Methodist Church.

However, although I had lived within easy walking distance of Whitley Hall until 1991, my home has never been in the Spring Gardens area of Reading and, consequently, I did not realise until I began my research that Whitley Hall had a predecessor which was still standing during my lifetime. I determined therefore that personal reminiscences should form the basis of this project along with other primary sources, such as minutes of meetings, deeds and maps as well as secondary sources like newspaper articles, entries from street directories, books and pamphlets. Since those with early personal memories were by then in their eighties and none of those had photographs of Spring Gardens Mission, it was obvious that no time should be lost if I were to obtain as detailed an account as possible of an area which, during its 150 or so years' history, had experienced great changes.

I therefore set to work on this investigation into the Spring Gardens area of Reading in 1989 and had achieved the basic structure and much of the groundwork when one of the couples, who had been invited to the 80th anniversary celebrations, returned to worship at Whitley Hall. Len Cook showed me a sketch of Whitley Pump which he had drawn from memory as a result of reading Bob Cooper's article *'Bobbing about in Whitley Street'* in the January/February, 1992 *Newslink*. From this developed the possibility of sketches from memory for which no photographs had emerged.

Spring Gardens Mission was the second Methodist Church to be built in Reading and, as I read and researched for this book, I began to realise that there was a difference between it and the first one. Wesley had started life in Queens Road, moved out of that area to Church Street and later returned to Queens Road. On the other hand, the move of Spring Gardens Mission to become Whitley Hall in 1906 meant that the congregation stayed within the same area of Reading, so, rather than concentrating just on Spring Gardens Mission and Whitley Hall Methodist Church, I chose to widen the study to include all aspects of the Spring Gardens area.

This seemed even more relevant when I discovered that there were very few references to that area in the existing literature. Even at the beginning of the third millennium (April 2000), there were no books about Spring Gardens in any of the libraries in Reading and only one book about the Whitley area (and that had been published 11 years before).

In 1996, the 90th Anniversary of the Church had been celebrated with another reunion of those who had been connected with its Sunday School. As for the 80th, people were invited to take part in the day's services and to lend photographs and other memorabilia for a display. From the photos, it was obvious that the Biblical quote from the book of Revelation chapter 22 verse 17 chosen to adorn the altar area of Whitley Hall Methodist Church:

LET·HIM·THAT·IS·ATHIRST·
COME· AND·WHOSOEVER·
WILL·LET·HIM·TAKE·THE·
WATER·OF·LIFE·FREELY·

was most appropriate for a Church in the Spring Gardens area of Reading.

However, perhaps the fact that, by 1950, the text had been changed to "O worship the Lord in the beauty of Holiness" was to be a foretaste of what was to happen in the area. Those words were taken from Psalm 96 verse 9 and are in the ninth hymn in the Methodist Hymn Book. Its fourth verse contains the line "Mornings of joy give for evenings of tearfulness". Certainly the Spring Gardens area is, in 2001, still experiencing its share of sadness.

As a tribute to all who have been connected with Spring Gardens Mission and Whitley Hall Methodist Church throughout their histories, especially those who have influenced my own life, I dedicate this investigation into the Spring Gardens area of Reading, Berkshire, England.

Chapter I: Springing Up

See! The streams of living waters,
Springing from eternal love,
Well supply Thy sons and daughters,
And all fear of want remove;
Who can faint while such a river
Ever flows their thirst to assuage -
Grace, which like the Lord, the giver,
Never fails from age to age?

Verse 2 of no 817 in Hymns and Psalms
by John Newton (1725 - 1807)

Having lived for almost the first 30 years of my life in the Basingstoke Road on the opposite side of the road to the Four Horseshoes Public House (which has been the Mongolian Barbeque since June 2000), it became a common occurrence to hear or to say:

"I'm going shopping. I won't be long. I'm only going to the top of Whitley!"

Now, although that expression was used to indicate that the person was going to Whitley Street, that street has not always been regarded as being in the area of Reading now known as Whitley. In fact, Whitley was originally a hamlet in the Parish of St Giles and it was not until *1882*, in the Smith's *Directory* of that year, that Whitley has an area designated as Spring Gardens. Certainly, in the very first edition of Webster's *Reading Directory (1874),* which appeared just after the renaming and renumbering of the streets, Spring Gardens appeared in the Reading street list. Other roads nearby, such as Boult's Walk, Martha Place, Milman Road, Tank Road, Whitley Crescent, Whitley Place, Whitley Road and Whitley Street also featured in the Reading Street List whereas Christchurch Gardens, Southern-hill and Whiteknights Park were in the Whitley Street Guide.

During that decade, according to Macauley's *Directory of Reading, 1871*, Whitley was a hamlet in the parish of St Giles and basically started just at the southern edge of the area chosen for this study. In Kelly's *Directory of 1909*, Whitley was still being mentioned as a hamlet and, as one of the contributors to this study summarised, when I told him that I was intending giving the book the title: *The Top of Whitley* - "There was no bottom then!"

Going back to the 1830s, Pigot's *Street Directory of 1830* has the entry:
"Button, Geo, Whitley Street, Spring Gardens", so we realise that Whitley Street was defined as being in the Spring Gardens area of Reading at that time. Work was, in fact, still in progress on the site and interesting pre-historic remains were continuing to be found. As an example, it was recorded in the *October 21st, 1833* edition of the *Reading Mercury* under the heading "Alluvial Remains" that, when a well was being sunk:
"in some ground in Spring Gardens in this town, the workmen on reaching a depth of about 30 feet met with a strata of shells embedded in a species of green sand but varying much from that in which the oysters were found at Katesgrove. One piece, which has been deposited by a member of the Philosophical Institution in the Museum (then at 36, London Street), is as interesting a specimen as any perhaps ever excavated. Some of the shells, which are a variety of shapes, have the original polish, others impressed in chalk display the minutest markings; while some, half open, exhibit the animal crystallised within. It is difficult to connect a period of 4000 years with the fresh appearance these shells manifest."

According to an article entitled *"The Whitley Conduit"* which was part of a collection compiled by William Tosland of Hillside, Spencers Wood under the heading *A Tour Around Reading 1920 - 1930,* the area was being written about as early as the sixteenth century. Then, during the reign of Henry VIII, William Grey of Reading wrote of the "barn and close called the Conduit Close wherein the spring's head is that serveth the King's House of Reading". The King's House was denoted as being the same as the old abbey, which, after its dissolution, became the property of the King. The article had described Conduit Close as positioned near Whitley Street: "The hamlet of Whitley now forming part of Christ Church parish has a notable history. Near the place where the trams stop there is a row of houses called Conduit Crescent and if the curious reader will walk down a short passage near these habitations, he will find the remains of the conduit that supplied Reading Abbey with water." He also commented that in 1739 a Reading historian had written: "Within the memory of man there have been several yards of leaden pipes dug up, which went under the river and conveyed the water from Conduit Close to the Abbey."

This is further confirmed by Leslie Davis, whose article *Interesting Reflections* in the *July/August 1988* edition of *Newslink*, states: "The point where Whitley Street curves into Christchurch Road was named Conduit Crescent, while near the top of Highgrove Street was Conduit Close within which was located the historic conduit fed by one of the many springs in the area reputed to possess miraculous powers. From this conduit water was piped through to the Abbey. Over the years lengths of lead pipe made at the Abbey plummery have been unearthed. Apart from their pious lifestyle the monks must, of necessity, have developed skills as civil engineers in constructing the conduit and routing the pipeline down to the Abbey."

It was that source of ready water that was eventually to prove very useful to a much wider clientele through the waterworks company. After an initial failure in 1694 when the engine set up in Mill Lane to pump water into the town centre had proved inadequate and was therefore abandoned, the civil engineer, William Cubitt, advised a reconstruction of the works in 1818. At that time, pumping machinery capable of raising 250,000 gallons a day was installed, a lofty tower was built in Mill Lane and also, a second reservoir at Spring Gardens on Whitley Hill. These improvements enabled water to reach the higher parts of the town, and no doubt led to the eventual development of the Spring Gardens area.

Five years before Cubitt's reconstruction of the water works, a map had been drawn of Reading which W M Childs used in his *Story of the Town of Reading (1905)*. His comments on it were that "nearly all the houses in Reading, as it was in 1813, lay within the space of which the churches of St Laurence and St Giles and Grey Friars are the corners. If we were to extend our limits a little we might say that, except for a few houses along Castle Street, almost all Reading in 1813 lay within a three sided figure whose base was Friar Street and whose two sides united on the top of Whitley Hill. One of those two sides was formed by the Market Place, London Street and Sivier Street (now Silver Street); the other by the Butts, Seven Bridges, Horn Street and Southampton Street. Outside these limits were the open fields." When he compared that map to the one drawn in 1610, he commented that they do agree as to the extent of Reading, but the earlier one, in particular, shows clearly that the chief part of Reading in those times lay on the northern bank of the Kennet.

In her book *The Story of Reading*, Daphne Phillips mentioned that, in the seventeenth century, suspected cases of the plague were removed to a crude isolation hospital, known as the pest house, in Conduit Close, off Whitley Street. By the end of July 1625, two more huts for the confinement of the sick had been built at Conduit Close and the council had paid out £5 for these and for a coffin to bury the dead.

A modern day view of Conduit Crescent with replica Whitley Pump-May 2000

The Governor of Reading, Sir Arthur Aston, had his fortifications of the town put to the test less than two decades later, when, in April 1643, Reading was besieged by Parliamentary forces commanded by the Earl of Essex. One of the fortified outposts was on Whitley Hill, this being the southernmost point of the town. Just outside the bulwarks crossing Southampton Street and Silver Street stood the strongly fortified outpost known as Harrison's Barn. It belonged to Thomas Harrison, the wealthy brewer who ventured so much in the cause of his king, but the Royalists were outnumbered in the Siege of Reading and were unable to defend the town against the invasion by the Parliamentarians.

With its ready supply of water and its defensive position, it does seem strange that the Whitley Hill area was not developed until the nineteenth century. However, if we consider the population censuses, we see that in the one undertaken by order of Cardinal Pole in 1555, the population of Reading was then only 2,500 so its boundaries did not need extension.

By the time of the first Official Census of Reading in 1801, the population had grown to 9,421. However, by 1841, it had more than doubled to 19,074 and, by 1881, it had more than doubled again to 42,056. In the next two chapters it will be seen that Reading's three main industries started between 1790 and 1822. Its railway, which connected it with other great centres, was opened in 1840. These events will have contributed to the town's growth then in much the same way as its present growth can be attributed to the recognition of its importance to "Silicon Valley".

Early in the development of the Spring Gardens area, there seems to have been controversy connected with Conduit Close in that it appeared in a table on page 2 of the *October 14th, 1833* edition of the *Reading Mercury* entitled:

Public Property in the Possession of Members of the Corporation

Tenants' names	Property	How held	Yearly rent £	s	d
Blandy J Jackson	Dwelling-house, Buildings & Land, Whitley Street, called Conduit Close	On lease for 99 years from Michaelmas 1825	21	12	0

On page three, a description of each of the properties was given, and details of the corruption seemingly exposed in high places. The following was written about Blandy's obtaining of Conduit Close:

"The 'Conduit Close' consists of two and three-quarter acres of land, having a valuable frontage of 600 feet to the Southampton turnpike-road, and upon some parts of it stood a large tenement, a small cottage, a very substantial brick building comprising a three-stall stable, large coach house, granary and loft and other buildings. This property was leased by the Corporation for 99 years from Michaelmas 1752 at a yearly rent of 4*l* 12*s* (ie £4 - 60 in our present decimal currency as the *l* stands for *lira*, which is the Latin word for *pound*, and *s* stands for *shilling* of which there were 20 in a pound) and two pullets, and Alderman John Jackson Blandy in the year 1824 became the purchaser of this lease. In the year 1825, the term of 26 years in the old lease being then unexpired, Mr Blandy obtained from the Corporation (again in silence and secrecy!) an agreement to renew this lease for the term of 99 years from Michaelmas 1825 at the yearly rent of 21*l* 12*s* (ie £21 - 60). In the year 1831 Mr Blandy put up a part of this property for sale by public auction, in eight lots, and apportioned the whole rent amongst them, reserving to himself the buildings on the northern side . . . At the time this agreement was made the buildings upon the land (which occupy a very small portion of it) were worth more than the whole amount of rent yearly; if the property subject to the old lease had at that time been brought to the market publicly, its admirable situation for building purposes, and its contiguity to Mr Blandy's freehold dwelling house and premises would have rendered it the subject of eager competition and produced a very high price for it.

"On reference to the Corporation diary it appears that during the time the negotiation for this new lease was going on, Mr Andrews (Mr Blandy's partner) was mayor, alderman and town clerk; and Mr Blandy himself was deputy town clerk and the legal adviser of the Corporation and also one of the chamberlains part of the time and Mr Andrews and Mr Wm Blandy (the brother) were chamberlains the remainder of the time; and it appeared furthermore that Mr Andrews, Mr Wm Blandy and Mr Blandy himself were members of the committee of leases who surveyed the property and proposed in favour of the new lease! It has subsequently been discovered that Mr Blandy's building speculation was a bad one and an attempt has been made to procure the removal of the Blue-coat school to Conduit Close (a most inconvenient situation for it)."

Later that same year, two burglaries in the area were reported in the *November 11th* and *December 28th 1833* editions of the *Reading Mercury,* and, to our eyes, it would possibly seem strange that food was the most-mentioned item stolen:

"On Tuesday night last some daring burglars broke into the house of Mrs Smith in Whitley-street by forcing the wash house window and removing the bolts of the door; they carried off two cheeses and 2 lbs of currants, and from the manner in which many articles were disposed of it was evidently their intention to have cleared the shop; but, being disturbed, they made off and climbed over a wall six feet high, close to which was a well, the lid of which they opened that their pursuers might fall in. The miscreants succeeded in escaping with their booty - The same night, the next house but one, Mr Goddard's was broken into, and the thieves succeeded in stealing two silver spoons and a purse containing 14s 6d; they effected an entrance by removing some brickwork and left the doors and windows wide open."

Similarly, just over a month later:

"The house of Mr Faulkner, in Spring Gardens, who keeps a small shop, was entered by the cellar window, by some predators early on Wednesday morning and three flitches of bacon and other articles were taken away."

According to W M Childs in *The Town of Reading During the Early Part of the Nineteenth Century*, the Municipal Commissioners had reported that there were no police in 1833 but that a force of about 13 watchmen was appointed by the Commissioners for Paving. This meant that prior to the institution of police a few years later (June 9th, 1838), the only night protection was the old-fashioned night-watchman "going his round and calling the hour and the weather."

This lack of police organisation and the slowness of communication facilitated every form of robbery. Within sight of Reading, coaches, horsemen and carriages were stopped and robbed, as was Mary Russell Mitford, the author of *Our Village* (1824 - 32). According to a report in the *December 3rd, 1842, Reading Mercury:*

"Miss Mitford, when returning in her pony carriage to Three Mile Cross, was attacked by ruffians on Whitley Hill!"

Almost eighty years later, horses were still to be seen on Whitley Hill though no ruffians were to be seen when the following photograph was taken in 1920 or 1921. Gertie Young thought it was of an outing of Whitley Hall's choir leaving the Church in Whitley Street. Behind the wagonette, which was drawn by two horses, is Whitley pump and, if you compare the present-day photograph on page 16 with the buildings in the background, you can match up the crescent-shaped brickwork on the left of Conduit Crescent. Another photo taken on the same occasion showed a wagonette drawn by just one horse.

Chapter II: The First Trickle

Why hast Thou cast our lot
In the same age and place
And why together brought
To see each other's face,
To join with loving sympathy
And mix our friendly souls in Thee?

Verse 2 of no 374 in Hymns and Psalms
by Charles Wesley (1707 - 1788)

The opening of Reading Station took place at the end of March, 1840. That building was then the furthest point north in the Borough of Reading, whereas, to the south of the borough, a new area of residential housing was being constructed. At the time of the building of the Great Western Railway and its expansion during the next decade, the Spring Gardens area of Reading grew up near the boundary of the Borough with the hamlet of Whitley.

Initially, it seems that the Spring Gardens area of Reading was considered to be in Mount Pleasant. By the time of Yorke's *Reading Street Key 1839* and Fernyhough's *Reading Directory 1841*, there are entries under both Spring Gardens, MOUNT PLEASANT and Whitley Street, whereas in Pigot's *Directory of Berkshire 1830*, there is an entry under bakers of: "Button Geo Whitly St, Spring Gardens". Even in the *auction details of John Boult's estate in 1849*, Spring Gardens is mentioned as "situate in Mount Pleasant".

As can be seen from the following entries in Fernyhough's *1841 Directory*, none of the houses in Spring Gardens and Whitley Street had then been numbered and there were very few inhabitants detailed for either road, viz.:

<u>Spring Gardens MOUNT PLEASANT</u>
T Kemp Esq
Mrs Body
Mrs Duncombe
T Boult Esq
Mr Brown

Whitley Street
Barkshire, baker & grocer
J Lovegrove, carpenter
D Wicks, beer shop
S Holding, shoe maker
Mr W Ing, collector of water rates, Whitley tank
Pearce, carpenter
Chesterman, beer shop
Pilgrim, undertaker

Interestingly, each of the residents in Whitley Street has a trade mentioned so it would seem that then, as now, the street was a main shopping area.

By the time of Snare's *Reading Directory 1842-3,* Spring Gardens and Mount Pleasant are mentioned separately with 19 and five names respectively, and the names of:

Body Mrs
Duncomb Mrs
Boult John, Gentleman

then appear in Whitley Street which had 22 names (including four in Conduit Crescent). Although it would seem odd that three of the Spring Gardens inhabitants had moved, a much likelier explanation becomes evident when consulting the *Tithe Map of the Parish of St Giles for 1840.*

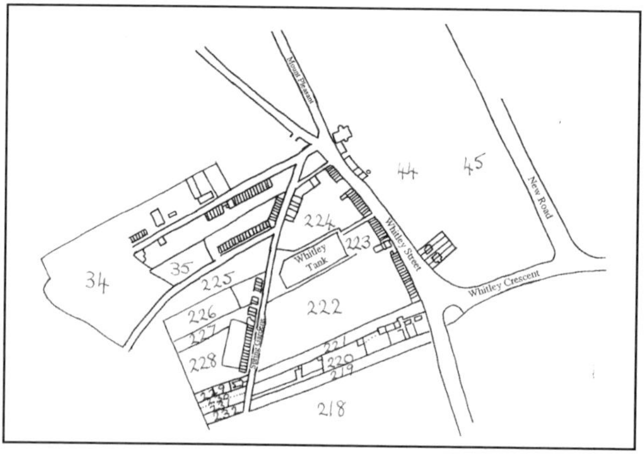

Plan of the Parish of St. Giles, Reading - showing ownership, occupation & cultivation of the land.

See opposite page for key

Surveyed by W H Fuller - Landsurveyor, Reading, 1840

There we see that the land owned by John Boult (219-221 & 229-232) extends from Whitley Street and over the road called Spring Gardens. This means that the address could be given as either Whitley Street or Spring Gardens. On the other hand, the land owned by Thomas Kemp (227 & 228) only fronts Spring Gardens. As well as showing ownership, the numbers on the sketch give an idea of the state of cultivation as well as that of occupation, the key being:

219(meadow)-221,229-232:	John Boult
217 & 218(arable):	Reverend Brown(but occupied by George Searle)
223 (water), 224 & 226:	Reading Water(but occupied by Joshua Hawkins)
227 & 228:	Thomas Kemp
222:	Mary Harris(but occupied by Blackall Simmonds)

Apart from the marked areas, the rest of the land was given over to gardens.

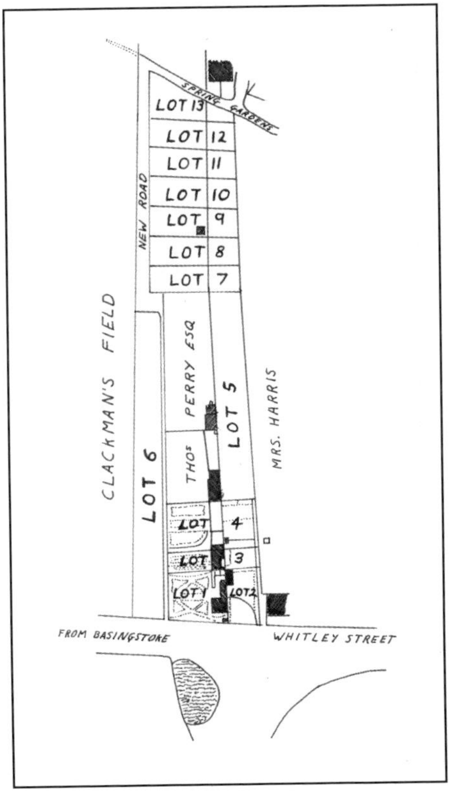

The *auction details* prepared by Haslams *under the direction of the trustees of John Boult's will*, after he died September 27th, 1848, throw further light on the problem. They tell us that, of the 14 Lots into which his land (shown as 219 and 220 on the *Tithe Map*) was divided:

"Lot 1 was late in the occupation of Mrs Body, deceased; Lot 3 is in the occupation of Mrs Duncombe, as yearly tenant, at an annual rent of £12 and Lot 4 is at present in the occupation of Mr Boult."

From the plan which accompanied the details, we realise why those three names could have been mentioned under Spring Gardens in one instance and under Whitley Street in another in the previous directories as John Boult's land stretches between those two roads.

So what is known about these early inhabitants of Spring Gardens? John Boult (1767 - 1848) owned 219, 220, 221, 229, 230, 231 and 232 on the *Tithe Map*, occupying the first two himself. He was referred to as a Gentleman in an indenture dated January 30th, 1840, but was previously a baker. The Mrs Body mentioned was his daughter, Olive Elizabeth Body (1800 - 1846), his fourth child, who had married Bernard Body of Shinfield but was a widow by the time of the previously mentioned entries in the Street Directories. Similarly, the Mr Boult is his fifth child, Thomas Griffith Boult (1805 - 1863) whose younger son, Francis John Boult, still owned property in Spring Gardens until his death in 1937.

Of the other two landowners, Thomas Kemp had obviously bought 227 and 228 for his own purposes whereas Reverend Brown had leased 217 and 218b to George Searle, who had also rented 218a from Mary Havell to use as arable and pasture land. In fact, much of the triangle bordered by Spring Gardens, Whitley Street and John Boult's land to the south was given over to market gardens (marked 222 and 224); water (Whitley Tank); and gardens (221 and 220), making way to meadow at 219 and leading to arable and pasture land owned by Rev Brown and Mary Havell. On the west side of Spring Gardens, there was again garden cultivation leading to market gardens from 226-5 and 34-5, the latter two being owned by Sir William George Milman, whose name lives on in Milman Road to this day, as indeed does John Boult's in Boult's Walk.

From those descriptions it is not difficult to imagine how Spring Gardens came to receive its name, there being both gardens and water in abundance in the area itself with meadows to the south and east leading to farmland.

By 1877, maps of the area were showing Whitley Street as being laid out with gardens and a fountain. There was also a spring marked behind Conduit Crescent as well as a pump and trough opposite Rose Cottage. Names such as Laurel Cottage and Laurel Terrace upheld the rural theme and Whitley Villa and Kingsclere Villa imply that there were still large houses in the area. However, names such as Essex Street and Waterloo Road seemed to be changing the image of the area somewhat. That is because the latter two have military connections as indeed had the renaming of the pub from The Green Man to The Wellington Arms.

However, we are racing ahead with undue haste and, as a result, are losing track of the composition of Spring Gardens and its first inhabitants. Snare's *Reading Directory of 1842-3* shows that, of the 19 houses having names by them, 13 also have numbers. Although three of the inhabitants are listed as being gardeners and one a gentleman, there are amazingly four beer shops (two of which are detailed as 'shopkeeper and beershop'). There was also a baker, a grocer and a coal dealer, plus a builder and a bricklayer. An even more interesting fact about those first inhabitants was that the three ladies are not credited with a Christian name, being listed only as Mrs. Of the 16 men detailed as occupiers, six had the Christian name John, four James and four Thomas. Samuel Ravenscoft, the grocer, and The Rev S Briggs must have helped the situation no end!

<u>Spring Gardens</u>

	(MOUNT STREET)
	Briggs The Rev S
1.	Wordsworth James
2.	Lukeman Mrs
3.	Herridge Mrs
4.	Halton John
7.	Messenger John
	Richardson James, Builder
	Netherclift James, Beer Shop
	Ravenscoft Samuel, Grocer
12.	Humphris Thomas, Gardener
13.	Berkshire John, Gardener
	SOUTH
13.	White James, Coal Dealer
25.	Hawkins John, Gardener
	SPRING GARDENS - KILN ROAD
	Herbert Mrs, Baker
1.	Faulkner John, Shopkeeper and Beer Shop
2.	
8.	Humberstone John, Shopkeeper and Beer Shop
9.	
	Kemp Thomas, Gentleman
39.	Burgess Thomas, Beer Shop
49.	Cave Thomas, Bricklayer

It is not surprising that people tended to be known by their surnames in those days as there were no repeats of those in Spring Gardens and only one in Whitley Street with a John Berkshire, gardener, at number 13 and a William Berkshire, baker, at number 10!

Another interesting fact about the early heads of household in the Spring Gardens area can be gleaned from the *August 18th, 1849* edition of the *Berkshire Chronicle*. There are disclosed the details of those who were eligible to vote for a Burgess to serve in Parliament for the Borough of Reading on August 7th and how they had voted (no such thing as a secret ballot in those days!). Four of those living in Spring Gardens voted for the Conservative candidate, John Frederick Stanford. John Faulkner, the beerseller, voted for the Whig, George Bowyer and Thomas Berkshire did not vote. Of the six, all were again blessed with Biblical Christian names, there being three named Thomas, a Joshua, a Benjamin and a John. Two of them were described as gentlemen, two as gardeners and there was a carpenter as well as the aforementioned beerseller.

The voting in Whitley Street followed a similar pattern in that seven voted for John Stanford, and the gentleman, J H Pierson, of Conduit Crescent did not vote. Similarly, there was another gentleman and two gardeners among the seven, but this time there were two bakers, a coachman and a bricklayer as well. The Christian names were not as Biblically based as in Spring Gardens, because, as well as two named Thomas, a Daniel and a James, there were also three named after Kings, two of those being William and one George. Incidentally, the numbers declared by the mayor on the morning following the election showed that generally, Stanford was the most popular:

Stanford	507
Bowyer	364
Norton	107
Number of persons who voted	978
Did not vote	250
Deaths and duplicate qualification	81
Total of members on the register for 1848-9	1309

As already mentioned, we have so far only considered the heads of household and, looking at the population figures for Reading in 1841, we see that St Giles Parish, in which Spring Gardens was situated, had a total of 6,737 inhabitants, being 3,144 males and 3,593 females.

Since there were 1,350 occupied houses, that works out at an average of five people per house. It is interesting that there were also 120 unoccupied houses and 27 being built in St Giles' parish, which was the same as St Laurence's and St Mary's put together. Of course, it is not known whether all the building was taking place in the Spring Gardens area, but the five occupied houses in Spring Gardens in 1841 had grown to 14 by 1847 whilst Whitley Street had similarly increased from eight to 28 (including those in Conduit Crescent).

By *1853*, Spring Gardens had 116 inhabited houses, according to Macauley's *Berkshire Directory*. Combining that information with the fact that the average occupancy of each house in the parish of St Giles in 1841 was five, we realise that there were around 600 adults and children in that road alone. In Whitley Street, there were 59 inhabited houses, which could have meant a further 300 people.

Quite obviously, those 900 or so inhabitants did not all arrive together, nor did their arrival herald the end of the growth of that area. As previously mentioned, maps from 1877 show that, not only had the building of houses started on the south side of Essex Street from number 1 to 55 by that time, but, there were plans to complete both sides of that road and join the terrace of 57 to 75 Essex Street with 59 to 73 Spring Gardens Terrace. There were also plans to continue Martha Place to form 1 to 15 Spring Terrace on the north side of the Reservoir by then.

Whereas the stretch of road from Christchurch School to Essex Street had been shown as being Tank Road on the 1877 map, the proposals were that it should be called Spring Gardens like the rest of the road. That and the previous proposals can be seen to have been adopted if we look at the map on the next page which was produced in 1899.

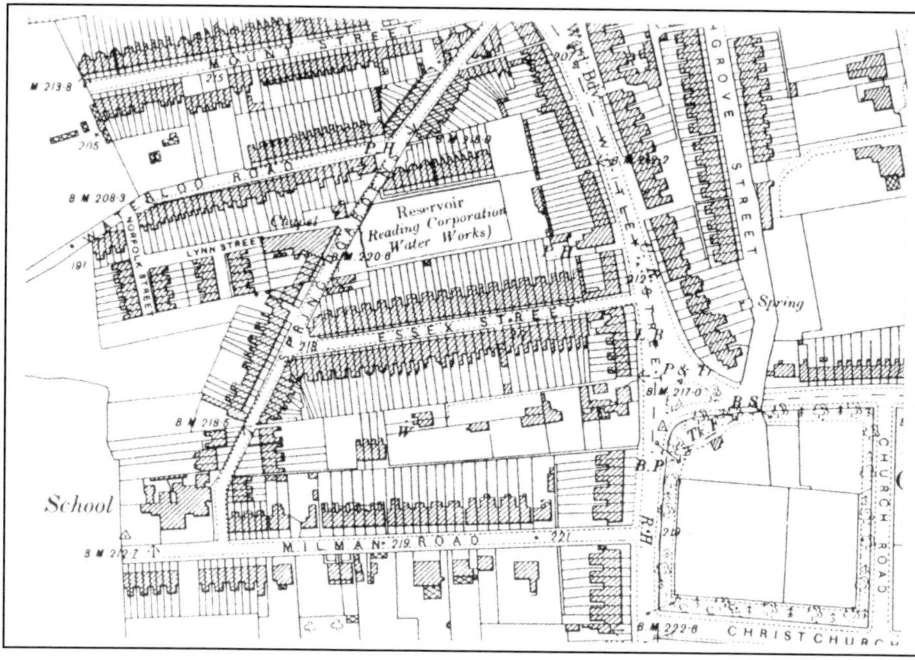

1899 Map of Spring Gardens area

As well as that proposed development, by 1899, the east side of Whitley Street had also been developed, as had Highgrove Street and Milman Road. The area behind the Methodist Chapel had also had houses built on it and Lynn Street and Norfolk Street had been named whereas Waterloo Road had had more houses built on its southern side.

As with all new Housing Developments, people moving into them require amenities as well as houses so the next few chapters consider facilities such as shops, public houses, churches, schools and recreational pursuits that were available to the early inhabitants of Spring Gardens.

Chapter III: On Tap

Give pure happiness in leisure
Temperance in every pleasure,
Holy use of earthly treasure
Bodies clear and spirits bright.

Verse 2 of no 341 in Hymns and Psalms
by Percy Dearmer (1867 - 1936)

Until the 1970s, Reading was renowned for its three 'B's - beer, biscuits and bulbs - as reflected in the present day naming of the restaurant in its Town Hall. The foundations of the latter-mentioned 'B' were laid in 1807 when John Sutton set up business in Reading as a corn and seed merchant. In the 1830s, his son, Martin Hope Sutton, an enthusiastic botanist and gardener, started a seed trial ground. He achieved such good results that, in 1837, he decided to set up his own business, persuading his father to join him under the title "John Sutton & Son" on the eastern side of the Market Place.

Like Suttons Seeds, Huntley & Palmers Biscuits owed its origins to a well-established but modest family business. In 1822, Joseph Huntley opened a biscuit bakery and confectionery shop at 72, London Street. On the opposite side of the road to the small shop was the Crown Inn, Reading's largest posting inn, which provided a ready market for selling the biscuits. Later, the link with the tin-making firm of Huntley, Bourne & Stevens meant further expansion so that a company, which employed 41 people in 1846, saw its workforce grow to over 5,000 by the end of the nineteenth century.

However, it was beer that was the first of the 3 'B's to become established in Reading and it is beer that has retained its link with the town to the present day. Reading's most famous brewery was founded in Broad Street in 1785 by William Blackall Simonds, but, by 1790, it had moved to a larger site in Bridge Street beside the river Kennet. Seven Bridges House (which was renovated as part of the Oracle development in 2000 and is now Reading College Business School) was then built to house the family beside their brewery. In those days, there were four other breweries in Reading, of which

Stephen's Brewery was producing 25,000 barrels of beer and porter annually.

By the 1830s, at St Giles' Poor-House, each man was allowed 21 pints of beer a week and each woman or child 10 pints, so it can readily be seen how beer was considered to be part of the staple diet at that time. However, the Poor Law Amendment Act of 1834 closed St Giles' Work-House, used St Mary's as the Poor-House for the Borough and converted St Laurence's into a Work-House for the Able-Bodied. From then, a rigid diet of two meals a day, the enforcement of strict discipline and little contact with the outside world were introduced to discourage the poor from applying for Work-House relief.

Against this background of beer appearing to be part of the staple diet at a time when the water was not considered safe to drink, it should not really surprise us to see, in the *1839 Yorke's Reading Street Key* and *1841* Fernyhough's *Reading Directory*, that four of the 12 inhabited houses in Whitley Street are described as beer shops. By the *1842-3 Snare's Reading Directory*, the total for Whitley Street and Conduit Crescent has dropped to two out of a total of 22 houses, but, by then, four beer shops are mentioned out of a total of 19 inhabited houses in Spring Gardens as well, thus confirming that the area had started to be developed between 1839 and 1842.

It is not until the *1847* Snare's *Berkshire Post Office Directory* that mention is made of an innkeeper in Whitley Street. Thomas Chesterman of the 'Green Man' is positioned between:

28	Parrin T H, Whitley School, and
31	Lovegrove John, carpenter,

so it would seem that the Green Man may have been the forerunner of the 'Wellington Arms' Public House, which is still in existence today. By the time of the Macauley's *Directory of 1859*, Mary Chesterman, presumably Thomas' widow, was shown as the innkeeper of the Wellington Arms, which is then numbered 30, Whitley Street. Since the first Duke of Wellington who had led the British army to victory in India and the Iberian peninsula, had died in 1852, the change of name no doubt resulted from that. Arthur Wellesley had been knighted for his negotiation of the peace in India in 1803, became Viscount Wellington in 1809, then Earl of Wellington in 1812, before being made Duke of Wellington in 1814 for his expulsion of the French from Spain. With his local connections, his name would, therefore, have been a popular choice for a pub's name after his death.

Tracing ownership of the Wellington Arms back, we see that, in *Snare's Reading Directory of 1842-3*, Thomas Chesterman's beer shop is shown between:

24 Pursey Benjamin, shopkeeper and
31 Lovegrove John, carpenter and joiner,

whereas the even earlier Fernyhough's *Reading Directory of 1841* has none of the houses numbered and gives initials for only four of the occupants of the eight inhabited houses.

This means that:

---- Chesterman, beershop appears between:
---- Pearce, carpenter and
---- Pilgrim, undertaker.

Previously, the beershop in that position had been owned by a G Phillips *(Yorke's Reading Street Key, 1839*).

Thus, it would appear that the Wellington Arms developed from one of the four beershops in Whitley Street and was first named The Green Man. Unlike the 'Prince Albert' in Spring Gardens, which is also first mentioned in the *1859 Macauley's,* its innkeepers stayed put, because, after the Chestermans' 20 or so years, James Noble followed them for at least the next 17, being mentioned in both the *1865 Macauley's* and *1882 Smith's Street Directories.* It was, in fact, the address that changed from number 30 in 1871 to no 70 in 1874 when the streets were renumbered and it is still numbered 70 - 72 today. However, after 1890, the Prince Albert also had stability of landlord, or licensed victualler, as they were then known, since William Stevens was there for approximately 15 years.

The Prince Albert, like the Wellington Arms had started life as a beer shop near Park Villa, which later became known as Park Cottage. It was in Spring Gardens on the corner of the road which became known as Waterloo Road.

This probably accounts for the fact that it was variously described as being 28 Spring Gardens and 1 Waterloo Road (*1884 Smith's*). In 1874, a third Public House, the 'Royal Victoria' came into existence at 28 Tank Road. At some time prior to that, the southern end of Spring Gardens, between Milman Road and Waterloo Road, had been named Tank Road (*1860 Macauley's*). This referred to the Reservoir and presumably wasn't at all connected with the expression 'getting tanked up'!, This third pub retained the same landlord, James May, from its opening until 1903 when Charles John Clarke took over.

By 1882, the part of Spring Gardens that had been known as Tank Road reverted to its former name of Spring Gardens, so, from that year onwards, Spring Gardens had the Royal William at nos 8 - 10, the Prince Albert at no 28 and the Royal Victoria at no 56.

Charles Gibson, who was born in 1921, spent his childhood living next door to the Royal William. He lived at 12, Spring Gardens, which he described as a "two up, two down, straight onto the pavement" house. He commented that the position of the house was very convenient for his father and his two uncles who all liked a drink! He recalled that "Mr Bowyer, who lived on the corner of Spring Gardens and Essex Street, had a haulage business which he carried on using farm carts and he used to stable his horses in the yard of the Royal William, as did Mr Williams and Bert Peck.

"Naturally, the stables led to the appearance of rats, so our dog, Spot, a little terrier, often earned my father a free pint by catching them for the landlord. One day, that same dog went missing, and, no matter where we looked for him, he was not to be found. Eventually, a man who had been busking in the area knocked on the door and asked if the dog which had been following him for most of the day as he walked down the middle of the neighbouring roads was our's. Sure enough, there was Spot, who, because his master (my father) played a mouth organ, had been attracted to the sound of the busker's instrument and followed him Pied Piper style! It must have made the busker's day as he was rewarded with 6d - no mean sum in those times - for returning Spot safe and sound.

"Mr Bowyer also had a lorry, with a canvas top and wooden seats along each side, in which he would take the men from the 'William' on various outings. I recall that there was a Thrift Club at the Royal William when Mr and Mrs Gaines were the landlord and landlady. Many pubs had similar arrangements to encourage their supporters to save for Christmas and for trips to places such as Riseley.

"There was also an annual Flower Show in the yard of the 'William' when sunflowers and marrows seemed in abundance. My father won first prize each year with his 'pair of marrows', which he grew on his allotment in Northumberland Avenue, where Reading Girls' School, formerly Southlands School, now stands. Mind you, what he didn't let on to the organisers was that he used a mixture of cottonwool and sugar to get both marrows to a similar size. Obviously, the vegetables were not edible after such treatment, but that did not matter when prizes were at stake!"

Charles mentioned that the fish and chip shop was run by Mr Otts, and it was a particular treat for him, in those days, to be able to sit on his doorstep and eat fish and chips, wrapped in newspaper. It was possible at that time to leave doors open, even when the family was out, and nothing would be taken. In fact, he remembered that people would call in with money when there was no-one in the house, and, when they called round later, would say: "Did you find that money I left for you on Tuesday?"

Charles recalled that the other pub in Spring Gardens, the 'Queen's', had, as its landlord and landlady, Mr and Mrs Froude who had a son, Pat, and a daughter, Dolly, plus a white bull mastiff. The landlord of the Wellington Arms, Mr Lyne, had a son, Bill, who was the landlord of Charles' father's house.

A photograph sent in by P Collier of Valentia Road to the *Midweek Chronicle* and published in its *August 9th, 1995 'Down Memory Lane'* feature, inspired responses from Mrs Niker and Dave Hutchins on August 23rd. The latter was one of the three men wearing bow ties in the photo. He played the accordian while Pat Froude (the son of the landlady of the Queen's public house at the top of Waterloo Road) played the piano and Bill Townsend the drums. He estimated that the photo was taken in 1936/7 at Christ Church Institute, Whitley Street and both he and Mrs Niker thought that it showed a party that had something to do with the Queen's.

Just a fortnight before – in the *July 26th, 1995 Midweek*, the landlords of the Wellington Arms in Whitley Street, Michael and Christine Power had been nominated as his favourite bar team by Callum Beveridge, who commented: "There is a great feeling here. We're like one big happy family". Michael reiterated that point when he said of the Wellington Arms: "This is a family pub in the true sense of the word. We attract parents and their children – people of all ages and that, I think, is what makes this such a homely pub. There is a lot more going on here than just beer drinking – good beer, I might add. We have darts and pools teams, for both men and women, live music on Friday nights and Sunday lunchtimes and we're hoping to introduce it on Saturday nights as well. And we regularly have charity nights. Our next venture is a charity darts evening on August 5 to raise money for an electric wheelchair; although I can't say more now because it's a secret".

The Wellington Arms in modern day Whitley Street, January 2001

Chapter IV: Opening the Flood Gates

Jesus where'er Thy people meet,
There they behold Thy mercy seat;
Where'er they seek Thee, Thou art found,
And every place is hallowed ground

Verse I of no 549 in Hymns & Psalms
by William Cowper (1731 - 1800)

The number of inhabited houses in Spring Gardens had grown in six years from 13 in 1847 to 116, and, those in Whitley Street from 21 (plus three in Conduit Crescent) to 53 (plus four) during the same period. By 1853, a Wesleyan Chapel is recorded as being between James Porter at 3 Spring Gardens and Daniel Tubb at no 5. Ironically, since at that time Methodists were teetotallers, the latter had a beer shop as his other neighbour and there was yet another beer shop just four doors away on the other side of the Chapel. Admittedly, there was also a road (later called Lynn Street) between those two.

We know very little about the creation of this chapel - the first indication of its existence is in Macauley's *Berkshire Directory of 1853*. However, from then onwards, it appears in each of the directories under Spring Gardens, although it is not mentioned in the *Non-Conformist Places of Worship* section of such directories until 1875 (in the first edition of Smith's *Reading Directory*) so it would be possible to overlook it unless one knew its exact location.

Despite the existence of the Wesleyan Chapel, which, by 1856 is also recorded as having a Sunday School, other religious groups in the town obviously regarded the Spring Gardens area as having much untapped religious potential. This is apparent from the *Saturday, August 26th, 1854* edition of the *Reading Mercury, Oxford Gazette, Newbury Herald & Berks County Paper*, where the first local item under Reading reads:

"Open Air Preaching: The adoption of this practice is becoming in many districts of the country much more general as appears by the notices in the provincial journals; in this town, the example of the Rev T Trench has been followed by the Rev J J Brown, the Baptist Minister; who for the last two Sundays has addressed an assembly at Spring Gardens, a populous district of this borough where it is to be feared many of the residents seldom approach a place of worship: the addresses are listened to with great attention and respect."

Although possibly small in number compared with other churches in the town, meeting as it did in a cottage where two small rooms were thrown into one and were immediately crowded, the membership of Spring Gardens Chapel remained extremely loyal to the cause. "Even the stairs were made use of for some of the tots", according to the *Souvenir of the 21st Anniversary of Whitley Hall (1927)* booklet.

In 1956, Rev Gordon Durrant in *Retrospect and Prospect* described in further detail how "A Sunday School for infants met in a cottage in Tank Road, while services for adults were held in Mount Street, where 'by the light of two tallow candles the preacher gave forth his message to eager listeners'."

When the debt which had hung over the first Methodist chapel in Church Street was cleared in 1867, 50 years after it was opened on January 17th, 1817, the Circuit took on a new lease of life. It seems that the purpose-built Spring Gardens Mission was one of the results in 1870, followed closely by the replacement for Church Street, the present Wesley Methodist Church in Queen's Road, in 1873.

That latter building, together with its schoolrooms, cost £7,250 and meant that the Methodist Society had returned to Queen's Road. The Wesleyan Home Missionary Department had sent Revs George Banwell and James Shoar to Reading in 1811 to see if they could restart Methodism, which had ceased to be represented there after 1804. The people had worshipped then in a building which had previously been a school so it became known as the Inkpen Chapel.

However, it is the second Methodist Society in Reading with which we are more concerned in this investigation and we do know that the original *Deed of*

Spring Gardens Chapel was dated February 10th, 1870. In the *Saturday, September 3rd* edition of the *Reading Mercury and Oxford Gazette*, we read:

New Wesleyan School Chapel, Spring Gardens, Reading

"On Wednesday, the foundation stone of this building was laid by J T Waterhouse, Esq of Honolulu, Sandwich Islands (now known as the Hawaiian Islands). The site of the Chapel is on a piece of land lately occupied by two cottages in Spring Gardens. For some years past a Sunday School, numbering more than 100 children, has been conducted by the Wesleyans under great disadvantages, owing to insufficient accommodation. The new Chapel is designed to answer the joint purposes of religious services and Sunday School. Mr S Whiting, of the Grove, is the builder and the entire cost, including the site, will be about 490*l*."

It is interesting to see that the letter "*l*", obviously standing for the Latin word "lira", was used rather than our present-day £ sign only 130 years ago. The same article tells us that 195 pounds had been contributed towards the 490 pounds total cost prior to that Wednesday and the total receipts on the Wednesday were 82*l* 18*s* 7*d* (ie £82 - 93 in our present currency), with over £40 being laid upon the stone. It was intended that when the Chapel was built, it would seat 200 people.

The stone-laying ceremony commenced at half-past three o'clock, and, among those present were the Wesleyan Circuit Superintendent, Rev C Hillard and his staff, also a Primitive Methodist Minister, Rev J T Penrose and the Trustees of the Chapel. After singing a hymn, the Rev S M Brough read the 84th and 132nd Psalms and offered prayer.

In his address, Rev Hillard commented that services had been held at that spot for 30 years past and "their friends wished to build a more suitable and commodious habitation. He trusted that the top stone would be laid with praises to God; that the house which they intended to build would far exceed in spiritual glory the old preaching room. He was glad that they had a native of Reading to lay the foundation stone - a son not only of a Methodist, but the son of a Methodist preacher. Mr Waterhouse's father (Rev John Waterhouse) was the instrument of building the Wesleyan Chapel in Church-street, and now his son was about to lay the foundation stone of the second Wesleyan chapel in Reading. (Cheers)."

The same article tells us that a bottle containing a statement of the building, a copy of the circuit-plan and a list of the trustees of the new chapel was placed in a cavity underneath the stone by the builder, Mr S Whiting. The treasurer, Mr Brown, then presented to Mr Waterhouse a suitably inscribed 'handsome silver trowel' supplied by Mr Botley, jeweller, King-street.

While laying the stone after applying the plumb-line, Mr Waterhouse recalled that in the spring of 1817 his father had laid the foundation stone of the Wesleyan Chapel in Church Street. Like many parents, he had not much to leave his children, but the one thing he had bequeathed to them was worth more than riches.

Spring Gardens Mission Hall, Lynn Street. Sketch from memory by Len Cook

It was to the schoolroom of the Wesleyan Chapel in Church Street that a large number of people adjourned for tea at 5 pm followed by a public meeting at the same place at 7 pm, at which Mr Waterhouse presided.

Although not identified as the Spring Gardens Mission, an article in the *January 7th, 1871* edition of the *Reading Mercury* obviously relates to that Church:
"A social Meeting was held in the new Wesleyan School Chapel on Wednesday evening. After tea, Mr Collins presided. The report was read by the Rev C Hillard. The debt on the building has been reduced to £35. Addresses were delivered by Messrs Chard, Beecroft, Whiting and Hensler."

In her history of the Reading and Silchester Circuit *As Stupid as Oxen*, May Ayres commented: "An enlargement in 1873 became necessary and an iron building was acquired. Throughout this time and in continuing years the work had been prayerfully maintained by a band of devoted workers and their missionary zeal had been of the highest order."

From the *Reading Yearbook of 1880*, we can see that services at Spring Gardens took place each Sunday at 10.30 am and 6.30 pm and on Wednesdays at 7.30 pm. It was also mentioned that the Sunday Schools met at 9.30 am and 2.30 pm where 118 scholars were taught by 17 teachers. The Society Steward then was Mr W Childs.

The *Souvenir of the 21st Anniversary of Whitley Hall* booklet tells us the names of those associated with the early days of Spring Gardens Mission:

"Mr Daniel Hensler, Local Preacher and Class Leader, was one of the earliest. After rendering splendid service he removed to Ashford, Middlesex, where he passed away at the ripe age of 97. He was a Local Preacher for 73 years. Another name is that of Henry Maggs, first Superintendent of the Sunday School; Mr Caudle and Mr Gladwell, also Superintendents." J J Beecroft was also mentioned as a Local Preacher and Mr and Mrs Wells as caretakers for 40 years. O M Payn was also Sunday School Superintendent for 20 years and Miss Franklin was organist.

It is always interesting to learn what our predecessors were doing a century ago and I found the *Reading Standard* particularly helpful in that respect. Since attention in 1991 had focused on pit bull terriers, it was most enlightening to read in the *March 13th, 1891* edition:

"On Saturday morning, while the 9 years old child of Mrs Mayers who lives at 64, Milman-road was playing in that road he was bitten by a small white dog with a dark coloured head. The same animal, which is supposed to be mad, bit the little boy of Mrs Munley of 94 Tank-road, in that thoroughfare. Both children were seen by Dr Guilding, who dressed the wounds."

Later that year it was reported on June 5th: "A bazaar was opened by Mr J Minty in the Wesleyan Chapel Schoolroom, Spring Gardens on Wednesday. There was a fair attendance throughout the afternoon as well as at the opening ceremony. The various stalls were presided over by Mrs Shepherd, Mrs Maunder, Mrs Flower, Mrs Nash and Miss Herbert. The proceeds are to be devoted towards religious work in Spring Gardens."

There is also evidence of the Spring Gardens Mission taking part in a town-wide event - the Reading Temperance Society's Annual Festival. In the *August 7th, 1891* edition of the *Reading Standard*, it was stated:

"The popularity which this festival has attained was again amply demonstrated on Monday, when despite the threatening state of the weather, it is estimated that upwards of 14,000 people (mainly children) assembled in Coley Park to participate in the different amusements. At half past twelve o'clock, the formation of a great procession of Band of Hope children was taking place, the greater bulk starting from West-street . . . In London-street division four was formed up, comprising St John's, Church-street, Trinity, London-street, Cumberland-road, Silver-street and Spring Gardens. These were conducted by the Rev G M Scott and at a time arranged were marched away to the top of King-street where they took up position at the rear of the preceding division (No. 3) . . . . The very small children were conveyed to the park in vans, these following some thirty minutes after the main procession. Arrived in the park the youngsters quickly found something with which to amuse themselves in the shape of swings, roundabouts, Harvard's Royal Crystal Palace Punch and Judy Show, which included chair balancers, boxers, plate spinners etc. Shortly after two o'clock the sports ring was surrounded by a numerous throng, all bent on witnessing the athletic sports open to members of the Bands of Hope attending the festival. Other very attractive items on the programme were the gymnastic displays at 2.30 and 5.30 by members of the Reading Lads Temperance Association. Gymnasium 'tricks' consisted of exercises on the vaulting horse, horizontal bar, vaulting bar, rings, trapeze, parallel bars, Indian clubs and bar bells. At 5 o'clock a large body of listeners assembled round the platform which had been taken possession of by the Reading Band of Hope Choir of 150 performers . . . Just over an hour later a temperance meeting was held on the same platform. The Bands of Hope partook of tea served by the committee early in the afternoon."

The *6th July, 1991 'Breakaway'* programme on *Radio 4* made the comment that the average distance travelled by a Briton in 1891 was only 17 miles a year as opposed to 17 a day in 1991. From that information, we can quite understand how important such events as the Temperance Society's Annual Festival were to the life of the inhabitants of the town.

The first records of meetings that have survived (despite being exposed to the elements after being stolen from Whitley Hall's safe) tell us that:

"A Society Tea was held on Wednesday, May 11th, 1892 in the Schoolroom and it is very gratifying to report that it was a great success as nearly every Member of the Church was present - we numbered about 54."
(*Minutes of Leaders' Meetings of Spring Gardens Mission*).

The reason for the good attendance at that social gathering can probably be realistically assessed from a comment made at the meeting held on *May 4th* that each Member should be specially invited by their Leader. We can also gain a little insight into social gatherings at that time from the description given:

"A Meeting was held after the Tea when we had an address from the Rev R W Little on 'Why am I a Methodist?', interspersed with singing and short addresses from the Leaders of the Classes and Officers of the Church, and a very pleasant and profitable Meeting was brought to a close by prayer and thanksgiving to our Heavenly Father for his love to us as a Church." It had previously been proposed that a collection be taken at the tables to defray the expenses, and that Mesdames Flower, Prior and Turner be asked if they would undertake the setting up of the tea with the help of as many friends as possible.

Now to those who do not have a Methodist background, terms such as Class Leader may need a little explanation if a better understanding of their implications is to be achieved. John Wesley's own experience of the love of God had come through meeting other people in groups for conversation, study and prayer. Wherever people listened to him, he formed them into societies and urged them to go on meeting after he had left them. They met in each other's homes and attended the parish churches on Sundays.

At Bristol in 1739, two societies decided to build a room on land which Wesley had bought in the Horsefair. It was opened in 1741 as a meeting house but it soon became a preaching place and it was there, in 1742, that the Methodist class system began. To raise money to pay for the New Room in Bristol (the oldest Methodist Meeting House), a Captain Foy suggested that the society should be divided into classes of 12 people and the Leader should collect from each member of his class one penny (1*d*) a week, thus giving a total of one shilling a week from each class. This not only provided a convenient way of raising money but also of looking after people.

It is interesting to note that that sum of money was still being collected at Spring Gardens Mission in 1894, over a hundred and fifty years afterwards, and possibly even later, as the *Minutes of December 12th* of that year state:

"Rev J R Sharpley nominated Mr Coppuck as a full Class Leader, because, at the beginning of the year 1895, several of his Class were going to be recognised as full Members and would begin to pay their 1d per week." However, by that time, the size of the classes was no longer strictly adhered to, because the first year for which records are available for Whitley Hall (the successor of Spring Gardens Mission) show us that, in the *April - July 1908 Circuit Plan*, the Class sizes were as follows:

11	Mr Morris
13	Mr Harris
38	Mrs T Rose
61	Mr Coppuck
13	Mr G Morris
44	Mr A F Olsen
10	Mr G Coppuck
190	

Mr Coppuck had been Leader of a Junior Society Class of boys which, in 1892, was meeting on a Tuesday evening, although from October 25th, 1893, their meeting night was changed to "Wednesday after the service". By December 18th, 1895, a second Junior Class of boys was formed.

That statement highlights two differences between Methodism at the end of the last century and now. During the 1890s, the four Wesleyan Methodist Churches all held midweek services as well as two services on a Sunday. Three of them had Junior Society Classes, which met weekly, as well as those for adults. According to the Circuit Plan, preachers were appointed to the Wednesday evening services as to the Sunday ones, so today's Ministers and Local Preachers have a much easier time of it than then! However, there is an entry in the *October 25th, 1893 Minutes*:
"The Secretary of the Mission Band (Mr G Morris) to make arrangements for the Wednesday Evening service when no preacher is appointed."

Another difference between the 1890s and the 1990s was that love-feasts were held a century ago. As an example, an entry for the *Leaders' Meeting of Wednesday, September 13th, 1893* reads: "also Mr Flowers (seconded by Mr Coppuck) proposed that a love-feast be held on September 24th, at the close of the evening service, carried."

We do not know much about the form those love-feasts took. The only other reference to them in that *Minute Book* was on *March 28th, 1894* when "Mr Hensler proposed, Mr Morris seconded that the Poor Steward in future provides a biscuit for the lovefeast, carried." In a later book, there is a reference on *Tuesday, October 30th, 1928* "It was proposed that a lovefeast be held at the close of the evening service on Sunday, December 30th, the Poor Stewards to be responsible for same." However, C R Moody who commented in his pamphlet *Lovefeasts - Records and Memories of an old Methodist Custom (1988)* that "one of the distinctive features of the various branches of Methodism during the first one hundred and fifty years was the practice of holding Lovefeasts . . . in general in this area (ie Yorkshire), the practice of having regularly planned Lovefeasts died out at the turn of the century."

John Wesley, following the example of the Moravians, had not hesitated to introduce the Lovefeast to his followers while at the same time discouraging his travelling preachers from administering the sacraments. Such Meetings of Prayer and Witness generally consisted of members (who had to show their membership tickets at the door) giving their testimonies to the Divine Grace after the bread and water had been served, a collection taken and an introduction given by the preacher. As Kathleen F Robinson commented in her *Introduction to Part II* of C R Moody's booklet: "Lovefeasts were begun so that ordinary Methodist believers could break bread together and share their Christian experience without the need for a Minister as in the Lord's Supper. Ministers were few and far between in those days." Certainly, Spring Gardens Mission does not seem to have been allocated a Minister in the 1890s, although the more centrally-situated Wesley and Oxford Road Methodist Churches were. In fact, apart from during its inception period, Whitley Hall also did not have an ordained Minister until 1938, as can be seen in the *list of Lay-pastors and Ministers who have served this Society of Methodist people* towards the end of this book on pages 151 - 153.

Special services were often held and, on *February 14th, 1894*, we read that Mr Coppuck reported in reference to the special services held by Mr Stacey: "we are thankful as a Church to our Heavenly Father for the manifestation of his Spirit in our midst as we have to report several additions to the classes also many was brought to a knowledge of the truth through these services."

On *December 18th, 1895*, it was proposed by Mr J Morris and seconded by Mrs Shephard that Mr Flower be asked to write to Mr Meredith in reference to conducting Special Services in this Chapel early in January. Mr Flower then proposed and Mr Coppuck seconded that a Week of Special Prayer be held the week before the special services.

Allocations of money from the Poor Fund were made to individuals whenever the Leaders met. Nowadays, money from the modern day equivalent of that fund, the Benevolent Fund, is mostly given to charities. Similarly, although the Minister and Class Leaders (who are now called Pastoral Leaders) may still request money from this fund for anyone in their class who is ill, bereaved or otherwise in need, they go straight to the Communion Steward in charge of the fund. It is only once a year that a special meeting is called to dispose of the remainder. The person in charge of Whitley Hall's Benevolent Fund until her death in 1990 had long-standing family connections with the

Spring Gardens area since her grandparents had been caretakers at Spring Gardens Mission for forty years. Sylvia Main (nee Smith) recalled for the *September/October 1989 Newslink magazine*:

"My grandmother, Mrs Wells (who had been widowed at 52) was caretaker of Spring Gardens Mission and lived at 44, Tank Road (later Spring Gardens). There was a way into Spring Gardens Chapel from the back of her house, which she would use when lighting up, etc for services and meetings. The lighting was gas and my mother, then a mere girl, with the help of her friend, Nellie Cummins (who later became a long-standing member of both Spring Gardens and Whitley Hall) would go into the chapel and light the gas lights with a long taper. Like most young people, they would have fun after doing their job playing hide and seek in and out of the wooden pews, some of which I believe are still with us at Whitley Hall in the Billiards Room.

"My mother's sister, Mrs J Stevens, was married at Spring Gardens and, like all the family, transferred to membership of Whitley Hall when it was opened. Her husband was a Church Steward at Whitley Hall for many years."

[Editor: 1) The pews remained until Whitley Hall was sold in November 1997 2) The aunt referred to by Sylvia in her final paragraph was Jessie who married Fred on June 7th, 1902, which happened to be his 25th birthday, I later discovered from their daughter, who became Kathleen Whitcher]

Apparently, the work prospered in its new home, which soon proved too small for the growing society. Further enlargements became necessary. During the ministry of the Rev W Briscombe, the final extension was made. As May Ayres commented: "Once again the numbers attending services became too great for the buildings and it became necessary to have a larger chapel. The last services were held in the old chapel in July 1897 and December saw the opening of the new building". The Rev W L Watkinson conducted the Opening Service, the subject of his sermon being 'The Palm and the Willow'.

As Rev Gordon Durrant commented in *Retrospect and Prospect*, "under the guidance of the Spirit of God, open air preaching, with singing led by the famous Spring Gardens Band, which toured the neighbourhood on Sundays and weekdays; class-meetings, prayer-meetings and preaching services brought the people in, and various enlargements and extensions to the building were carried out. At last it became clear that the Lord was leading these people to much bigger things for His Church and His Kingdom."

Until 1997, a list of 65 children and others, who had collected half a guinea (ten shillings and sixpence which is now equivalent to 52.5 pence) towards the building of Whitley Hall, was displayed in its No. 2 Vestry. After seven foundation stones had been laid, they had laid bricks at the stone-laying ceremony in July 1905, which, according to the *July 12th, 1905* edition of the *Reading Standard* "took place in brilliantly fine weather, the scaffolding had been gaily decorated with flags and bunting to mark the occasion; the Spring Gardens Band attended in uniform, and the Boys' Brigade attached to Elm Park Hall paraded on the site under Captains Olsen and Brown."

The last service in Spring Gardens Mission was conducted by Mr J Meredith. At the close of that service, the congregation joined hands and sang the verse:

> High Heaven that heard that solemn vow,
> That vow renewed shall daily hear.
> 'Til in life's latest hour I bow,
> And bless in death a bond so dear.

Even after the Spring Gardens Chapel members had moved to new accommodation at Whitley Hall in 1906, the building that had once housed the church later had its links with Methodism, and especially Whitley Hall, re-established in that one of its members, Richard Painter, a pattern maker, worked in what was once its Schoolroom. A C Cox owned the property then and Dick was a junior partner. He had married Rose Waite, whose grandfather, Mr Meredith, had preached the last sermon at Spring Gardens Mission before the first services were held at Whitley Hall. Rose and Dick still had what was the workshop clock in their lounge when I visited them and Dick recalled that the old chapel had later become a general corner shop.

Raymond Searle, whose parents were lifelong members of both Spring Gardens Mission and Whitley Hall, mentioned that he obviously could not remember Spring Gardens Mission as such but he did recall visiting the building as a boy, when it was a carpenter and joiners workshop, to collect bags of wood shavings to fuel the copper fire at home.

Chapter V: Educating the Off-Spring

We bring them, Lord in thankful hands
And yield them up to Thee;
Joyful that we ourselves are Thine
Thine let our children be.

Verse 3 of no 588 in Hymns and Psalms
by Philip Doddridge (1702 - 51)

Long before the State took responsibility for general education, the Church provided schools for the people. Ever since John Wesley founded Kingswood School in Bristol in 1739, Methodists have been involved in education and nearly every Methodist chapel had a school attached where general, as well as religious, education was given on Sundays.

Between 1840 and 1870, the Wesleyans built over 800 schools and two training colleges for teachers - Westminster College in Oxford for men (1851) and Southlands College in London for women (1872). After the Education Act of 1870, which set out to provide state education for all, the Methodists decided to hand over their schools to the state. A century later, only about 50 day schools and a dozen residential schools had been retained under their direct control, according to Jim Bates in *The Methodist Church*, which was published in 1977.

It seems likely that it was at the beginning of the boom period of 1840 - 1870 that the Wesleyan School Chapel was started in Spring Gardens. This is because the article describing the 'New Wesleyan School Chapel, Spring Gardens, Reading' in the *Saturday, September 3rd, 1870* edition of the *Reading Mercury and Oxford Gazette* stated: "They had held services there for thirty years past". In the *Street Directory of 1853*, a Wesleyan Chapel is mentioned at 4, Spring Gardens but it is not until the next available *Directory* - that of *1856* - that the description is given as :

Spring Gardens: 4… Frost Mrs A…Wesleyan School

Since the terminology remains similar after that and the word 'school' appears in each available directory (except that of 1874), it is possible the school was in fact started in 1856, although we have no direct evidence that that is so. It could have started before then since Christchurch School, which was built in 1868, does not seem to have received a mention in directories until the *1871 Macauley's.* The Sunday School was first given the prefix, Wesleyan, in the *1865 Directory* when the name of the road had also been changed to Tank Road.

As we read in the previous chapter, the foundation stone for the new chapel was laid on August 31st, 1870 and, in the *directory* of that year, "5 Tank Road" is shown as empty. This ties up with the description in the article that the new Wesleyan School Chapel is "on the site lately occupied by the two cottages", namely numbers 4 & 5 Tank Road.

In 1871, the site was described as "Wesleyan Sunday School and Chapel" and was between 1 and 17 Tank Road. Also, in that year, an article appeared in the *September 9th* edition of the *Reading Mercury*, under the heading of Wesleyan Sunday Schools. In the article, as well as mentioning that the newly-appointed superintendent of the Reading circuit, the Rev G Penman of Newport, preached two sermons in Church-street chapel on the Sunday, the Rev J F Stevenson gave an address to the schoolchildren in the afternoon. During the annual society meeting on the following Tuesday, at which Mr T Blackall presided, Mr Beecroft read the report which stated that "in the united schools of Church-street and Spring Gardens, there are 356 children and 47 officers and teachers."

In the *Yearbook of Historical, Statistical and General Information for Reading, 1880*, the Sunday Schools at Spring Gardens Chapel are detailed as meeting at 9.30 am (ie before the morning service which was then held at 10.30 am) and 2.30 pm. At that time, there were 118 scholars with 17 teachers - a teacher: pupil ratio of 1:7.

The first Church records that mention the Sunday School are the minutes of a *Leaders' Meeting* held on *January 27th, 1893*. From those, it is obvious how important the Sunday School was considered to be in the life of the Church as the only appointments made by Rev R W Little were:

Poor Stewards	-	Mr Flower and Mr Franklin;
School Committee	-	Messrs Hunt, Hensler, Morris Senior, Morris Junior, Franklin, Flower, Nash.

The latter were, in fact, all the members present at that meeting, apart from Rev Little. In the *Souvenir of the 21st Anniversary of Whitley Hall, formerly Spring Gardens Mission* booklet, we see that Daniel Hensler was a Local Preacher for 73 years before he moved to Ashford, Middlesex, where he passed away at the ripe old age of 97. James Morris was the first Bandmaster and John Morris, George Flower, A Nash and Mr Franklin are all mentioned as having been associated with the early days of "Spring Gardens". In that same booklet, Henry Maggs is mentioned as being the first Superintendent of the Sunday School; Mr Caudle and Mr Gladwell also as Superintendents and O M Payn as Sunday School Superintendent for 20 years.

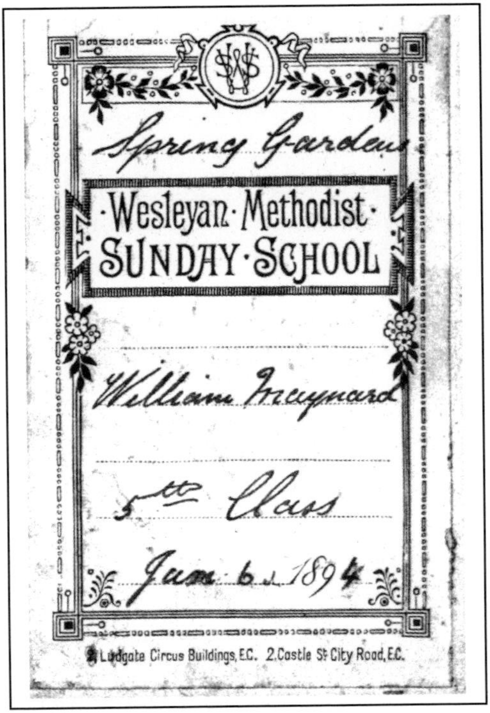

Similarly, the first Circuit Plans now available also date from about the time of the first Church records. In a *Circuit Plan for the Wesleyan Methodist Church -Reading Circuit*, as it was then known, there is mention in the *April 8th to July 1st, 1894* edition under the heading 'Specials' of Spring Gardens Sunday School Anniversary on April 29th. Obviously, the practice of arranging special Anniversary services, as recalled by later scholars in chapter X11, was already well established by 1893.

Another custom also firmly established by then was the giving of books as prizes for attendance at Sunday School as can be seen from this label in a book entitled *Jim and his Charges* by Alice Briggs. It was published by the Wesleyan Methodist Sunday School Union and was presented to William Maynard in 1894. The book is still in the possession of his son, Bill Maynard, who was one of my next-door neighbours when writing this chapter.

However, there are some differences because, in the *Minutes of the Leaders and Stewards Meeting* held at Spring Gardens Mission on *October 2nd, 1905*, it was "proposed that a subcommittee be formed consisting of the two Society Stewards, the two Sunday School Superintendents, two Secretaries and Mr G Coppuck as secretary and convenor, in connection with Children's Sunday and the week's Mission following." The nearest to such an event during my lifetime was the 1954 Student Campaign when I particularly recall learning choruses with actions in their Sunshine Corner held in the Large Schoolroom at Whitley Hall. However, for others, it proved a much more momentous time as Rev Michael N Winch, now a Minister at Newbold Baptist Church in Rochdale, remembers that as the time when he first responded to Christ. Just prior to the closing services at Whitley Hall, he wrote on October 27th, 1997:

"I was brought up in Whitley Hall where my grandparents (George and Minnie Winch) were founder members from the former Spring Gardens Mission. My own parents, Walter and Ada Winch, were very active, with my father serving as assistant organist for many years then assuming the position of organist, in succession to Mr W Jelly, in 1950 until his death in 1979.

"My mother was remembered for her many plays performed either in the Large Schoolroom or as part of Christmas services in Church. She was much involved in Coffee Mornings from their inception and in fundraising efforts such as the Garden Parties in Christchurch Vicarage grounds and then at Whitley Glebe. In 1986, she moved to Kenilworth to live closer to my brothers, Nicholas (Nicky) and Geoffrey, then, after a stroke in October 1996, she moved to a nursing home in Coventry.

“I remember with gratitude my times in Whitley Hall Sunday School. Teachers such as Mrs Jane Joy, Mr Bertrand Purnell and Mr Stanley Morris were people in whom I saw the love of God expressed. In September 1949, the Rev W Beddard Smith came as minister and, together with his wife, he started, in January 1950, a Young People’s Fellowship on Sunday afternoons for those too old for Sunday School. Later that year, he was photographed (see opposite) helping in the renovation by voluntary labour of the Church ready for the grand re-opening on Wednesday, July 19th, 1950. On that day, a divine service at 4 pm was followed by a public tea at 5.15 pm, a musical interlude and community hymn singing at 6.30 pm and a great Thanksgiving Rally at 7.15 pm.

“Those were formative years in my life and, from the seeds sown by Sunday School teachers and the YPF ministry of the Smiths, I came to Christ during the April 1954 ‘Student Campaign’ in Whitley Hall. Following on from that, Mr Bernard (Tom) Law started a Young People’s Christian Endeavour group to help nurture us ‘new Christians’. There I learned to pray publicly and to give brief talks. With the encouragement of Rev Gordon A Durrant who arrived in September 1954, I began both Sunday School teaching and local preaching and became a fully accredited Methodist Local Preacher in 1958.

“After two years National Service in REME, God’s plans for my life developed along lines different to my expectations. This led to ordination in 1977 and currently I serve as part of the pastoral team at Newbold Baptist Church, Rochdale, Lancs as well as having a wider itinerant Bible teaching ministry in Britain and South India.

“It was a special joy to preach at the 90th Sunday School Anniversary in May 1996 leaving me with fond memories of what was to be my last visit to Whitley Hall, the Church that played such an important role in the plan and purpose of God for my life. I give God the glory for the privilege of having been part of Whitley Hall Methodist Church.”

Michael’s mention of his mother’s many dramatic productions in both the Church and the Large Schoolroom reminded me of occasions when I took part in some of them. On one occasion I had a real life carpenter as Joseph when I was Mary. Clifford Hunter taught woodwork at Hugh Faringdon RC School in Southcote and then at Reading College and, from that day until he died, he always called me Mary on the strength of that play. Mind you, Ada must have had quite a few last-minute problems with producing plays as I can remember the pantomime "Snow White and the Seven Dwarfs" in 1962 when I was rushed into hospital with appendicitis. I had been at the usual rehearsal on the Monday evening but was taken into the Royal Berkshire Hospital later that same evening and operated on the next day. After convalescence at Peppard, I came home a week Wednesday afterwards so was able to watch the performance on Thursday, March 15th, only to hear that another member of the cast – Brian Simms - was then in hospital with peritonitis!

Naturally, there is no one alive today who remembers the Spring Gardens Sunday School. However, Sylvia Main, whose grandmother, Mary Ann Wells, lived at 44 Tank Road and was the caretaker of Spring Gardens Chapel, recalled for the *September/October 1989 Newslink* that her grandmother had told her how a "Mr Harry Giles held Sunday School in the kitchen of the old Chapel and would sit quite a few children around, even on the edge of the stone copper where the water for teas etc would be heated."

The Anglicans had, of course, been building schools prior to the Methodists, so even though Spring Gardens Wesleyan School preceded Christchurch School, the latter was the first purpose-built school in the Spring Gardens area. The total cost of the school buildings and the headteacher's residence was £2,174, for which the Government provided £490, the Diocesan Board £50 and the National Society £150. The remaining £1,484 came from local subscriptions and collections. The Christchurch National Schools, as they were then called, were only a five-minute walk from Christ Church (itself only built in 1862 and consecrated on August 7th of that year) and were founded in Milman Road in 1868 for 381 children.

In the *January 28th, 1871* edition of the *Reading Mercury*, it was mentioned that 190 children were in attendance at Christchurch National Schools and 37 attended the Night School held there. Later that year, in the *November 25th* edition of the *Reading Mercury*, it was recorded that, "on the Wednesday evening, a very successful concert in aid of the funds of Christ Church Schools was given in the schoolroom, Grove-road, Whitley."

In those early days, children were punished far more severely than they are today. As an example, on July 30th, 1868, Walter Chippen was caned for throwing clay. Other crimes that merited caning included: "Being careless when doing their addition sums", having dirty hands, spending their school money, as well as the more obvious truanting and stealing. In the case of the latter, the caning was often a flogging as happened in February 1885 when "one Roderick Smith stole some money from the boxes in the school last week. The vicar came and spoke to the boys and Smith was flogged after School, being given 12 stripes." The next day, "Henry Bloomfield, to whom Smith gave some of the money, was flogged - 8 stripes."

However, it was not all punishment for those early children as J H Wilson, Esq paid for the whole school to see WOMBWELL'S MENAGERIE in 1869 and, in fact, he and Mr Attenborough gave the school several "Treats in their grounds". A half-day's holiday was given on November 4th, 1891 for the opening of Palmer Park while, ten years later, a holiday was given to celebrate the return of the Berkshire Volunteers from South Africa. Another 'special' occurred in 1902, when the school closed at 9.15 am for the visit of the Prince and Princess of Wales to Reading.

On September 4th, 1891, the Free System of Education had begun, so, by the time of the Kelly's *Directory of Reading, 1909*, the school had 564 pupils with an average attendance of 514. H L Gilbert Heath commented:

"I lived at School House, 66 Milman Road from 1908 until 1950. This house was the former home of the headmaster of the Christchurch Schools Boys' School. To gain admittance to this we had daily to cross the school playground at the bottom of Milman Road via an iron gate, a hazardous procedure when the boys were all at play. To that extent therefore, I suppose I could be reckoned as someone who had knowledge of Christchurch School."

It will be noted that Gilbert referred to the Boys' School and, in fact, when the Christchurch National Schools were opened on July 14th, 1868, there were three schools in the one building - Infants', Boys' and Girls'. It was not until April 1st, 1927 that Christchurch Junior Mixed and Infants came into being after the retirement in 1926 of Mr Ganderton, who had been headmaster of the boys' school for 40 years; and of Miss Lear in 1927. Although Miss Lear had not been headmistress of the girls' school as long as Mr Ganderton served in the boys' school, her teaching association with the girls' school started on January 12th, 1883 when she became an Assistant Mistress there, having been a Pupil Teacher for three years.

L Deadfield sent in a photograph of a class from Christchurch School, Spring Gardens along with a letter to the *Midweek* and it was published in the *Wednesday, November 22nd, 1989* edition of that paper. As well as mentioning that the photograph was taken in 1922, he described how Johnny Stevens was best remembered because: "his mum would come to her front door and shout to let us know the first or second bell had rung at the school, telling us to hurry or we'd be late. We would be far too busy in the Tank in Spring Gardens playing football or cricket to hear a bell.

"One afternoon about 20 of us were late after the second bell because the two sides were more interested in trying to score a winning goal. When we did arrive at school and were allowed in, we were lined up in front of those who were in class and firmly dealt with by our headmaster, Mr Samuel Ganderton, who could wield a cane quite well!"

At the time of the changeover on April 1st, 1927, the older children were drafted to Secondary Schools and Miss Irene Lamport Gilbert began her duties as head of Christchurch Primary. It was during her time as head that Charles Gibson was a pupil at the school prior to his transfer to Katesgrove School at the age of 11. He remembered that the all-female staff then consisted of Miss Eason, who was the pianist, and also the Misses Deacon, Goodie and Soanes. Similarly, he recalled that there was a teacher who had a hearing aid of the type commonly used at that time. If she could not hear what a pupil said, she would bang her chest (presumably to obtain a better response from the aid) and enquire: "What did you say, boy?"

Another incident that stuck in his memory from that period was connected with the Tank. Apparently, this tended to flood during wet weather and, at such times, the children were told to go straight home from school, not stopping to play in the Tank as they liked to do. Charles and a friend decided to ignore that advice and went as usual since, by then, his family had moved to Spring Terrace, which bordered the south side of the Tank. The next day, when the whole school was assembled in the hall, the pupils were asked if anyone had stopped off at the Tank on their way home the previous evening. Eventually, since no one admitted it, Charles' name and that of his friend were called out. Naturally, they still maintained their innocence but were caned nevertheless, not because they had been in the Tank, but for telling lies!

Charles recalled that there was a Boys' Section of the Spring Gardens Band at Christchurch School when he was a pupil there and, as a result, he learnt to play the trombone, then the cornet. He was also taught to play the piano by a Miss Humphries who lived in Milman Road and used to hit his hand when he made mistakes. However, although he still retains an interest in music - he plays his electronic organ every day now - in those days he preferred "going out to play" with his friends when they called round for him. Practising his instruments did not hold such a great priority in his life then!

As a result, despite the efforts of George Watkins, the conductor of the Spring Gardens Band who had started the boys' section of the band at the school, he did not go on to become a member of the band itself, although some pupils did. Apparently, George, whose dance band used to play at the Majestic Ballroom in Caversham Road, had started the band at Christchurch School as a preparation for boys to join the Spring Gardens Band later and a Mr Pendery of Great Knolly's Street helped him in the teaching of the trombone.

Bob Russell, who remembers the School from about 1937 – 1944, was able, in a letter of 15th February, 2000, written in Derby where he now lives, to throw more light on the four members of staff mentioned by Charles Gibson. He commented that the headmistress, Miss Lamport-Gilbert, lived in Liebenrood Road whereas Miss Soanes, who taught music, lived at 3 Milman Road with Mr and Mrs James Collins, the former of whom ran a gents outfitters' shop in Whitley Street. The deputy head, Miss Eason, taught music, needlework, PT (Physical Training), games and cricket and Miss Goody retired in 1942, having spent her entire teaching career at Christchurch School.

Despite his comment that the staff revealed nothing of their private lives nor interests, he also mentioned Miss Hogarth, who taught the Infants and left to go to Bristol, but was then believed to have been killed in the Blitz. He knew that two teachers lived with their parents - Miss Boyles who taught years 1 and 2 impressed him by travelling in from Thatcham each day on the Thames Valley bus to the station and a trolley bus to the school. Similarly, Miss Nobbs travelled from Wilderness Road by racing bike – a mina 'maverik' – to teach boys' craft lessons. However, he did comment that the idea of them having a 'significant' friendship or a sex life was unthinkable!

Bob's impression of the staff was that they were a very formal sisterhood: "We never knew or even heard of their Christian names! They always dressed correctly in pale, pastel colours, undemonstrative clothes and 'sensible' shoes. Both the head and deputy head were obsessed with 'tone' and did not approve of contemporary culture or the mores of the cinema nor what was then 'pop' music or entertainers. As a result, there were a few schools' radio broadcasts but they were used with extreme discretion.

"The only men who entered the school were the vicar, who often came on Fridays to take assembly, the attendance officer and a part-time games master to take Standard III and IV boys for football in a playing field in Northumberland Avenue. The caretaker, Mr Dyer, who lived in Milman Road, was the only full-time male role model. He was a man of unremitting duties, lighting coal fires and clearing up messes left by the incontinent!"

As with many youngsters, it is the playground that figures highly in their minds about their schooldays and so it was with Bob when he wrote to the then headmaster of Christchurch Primary, Peter Stagg. Peter forwarded the article to the editors of *Newslink* and it appeared in the *July/August 1995 edition*:

"My Junior School, Christchurch, Reading, had two playgrounds. The boys' playground overlooked part of the last two miles of the Kennet and Avon Canal. It looked down a steep clay bank, known locally as 'the Banks', across a disused brickyard to the canalised stretch of the River Kennet. Across the river stood the CWS (Co-operative Wholesale Society) Preserves factory, 'the Jamo', dominated by a tall brick chimney and a grey concrete water tower. A large timber yard was also nearby and the GWR had a marshalling yard, where a resident tank engine together with a shunters' platform appeared to play with trucks and wagons all day long. Occasionally another engine would arrive and remove the assembled train up to the main Reading, Newbury and

West Country line, a few miles away. The foreground and distance consisted of the water meadows flood plain of the Kennet, the only distant building being the brick engine house and chimney of Fobney Pumping Station.

"In those years, a long time before the Kennet and Avon was even partially reopened, the appearance of a barge or small motor boat was an event of some significance. Usually, these were dredging or maintenance craft working to retard winter flooding. The canal path up to Fobney and Burghfield was the haunt of anglers and walkers.

"Little did I know in those years that I was watching over what remained of an early Victorian 'dream' of a seaway between London and Bristol that could have rivalled some of the world's great ocean-linking canals. In 1830 there was talk of a ship canal that could take vessels of 400 tons, and 8 million pounds (a vast fortune in those days) was budgeted for its construction.

"This was to have been the fulfilment of the work of those who first excavated the canal between Reading and Newbury in 1723. John Rennie extended this in 1810 as far as Bath. His canal was 40 feet wide, could take barges 70 ft in length carrying up to 60 tons. It had 79 locks and cost about £1 million. It was an immediate success linking Reading, then a town with a population of 10,000, with Bath, Bristol, Birmingham and Staffordshire. Prices fell owing to reduced transport costs and there was much Bristol to London through-trade. With the introduction of narrow 'fly' barges, goods could be transported from Bristol in five days in summer, six in winter. This period of prosperity was short-lived. The Great Western Railway came. In 1852, the GWR bought the canal, and, by 1906, there was hardly any through traffic. The dream of the great Sea-Way: London – Bristol – New York had died.

"The riverside meadows, trees and wildlife had the waterway more or less to themselves. With dereliction came peace and tranquillity. It is to be hoped that the newly emerged recreational canal users will deal kindly with the environment and regard the 79 locks as a reminder of engineering visionaries of the past. I wonder if small boys still watch from the playground fence and think about the Sea-Way that never was!"

The school gained 'Controlled' status in 1948 when the Vicar was the Rev E Knell, MA who later became Bishop of Reading. G M Luxton, who became headmistress in 1950 and wrote in the *centenary year* booklet *(1968)* "Visitors have often commented on the happy atmosphere of our school", would no doubt be pleased to know that that was my impression when I visited Christchurch Primary in October 1990.

The children spontaneously spoke to me and when I said that it was my first visit, one of them offered to show me the plans of the alterations that were then taking place. These were on public display in the Hall and I later discovered that the work should last 56 weeks. As well as those plans for the future, the school seemed just as proud of its past as its then headmaster, Peter Stagg, commented about the old pupils who still return, even from abroad, to their 'roots'. He showed me the wall where children of yesteryear used to sharpen their writing implements in the days of slates.

New Christ Church C of E Primary School, Spring Gardens in January 2001

Chapter VI: And the Banned Played On

Lord, we know that Thou rejoicest
O'er each work of Thine;
Thou didst ears and hands and voices
For Thy praise design;
Craftsman's art and music's measure
For Thy pleasure
All combine.

Verse 3 of no 484 in Hymns & Psalms
by Francis Pott (1832 - 1909)

The only present-day reminder of the Spring Gardens area of Reading is no longer directly connected with that area. Members of the Spring Gardens Band are now drawn from all areas of Reading whereas, when it was first formed, all lived near the Spring Gardens Mission to which it was not only attached but was a very integral part of the evangelistic approach of that Wesleyan Methodist Chapel. It has already been mentioned in the previous chapter that, in the *Minutes of the Leaders' Meeting of Spring Gardens Mission* on *Wednesday, October 25th, 1893*, it is recorded: "The Secretary of the Mission Band (Mr G Morris) to make arrangements for the Wednesday Evening service when no preacher is appointed."

As with the early days of the church, we do not know very much about the band during its days at the Spring Gardens Mission, except for gleanings from the *Methodist Times.* As an example, in the description of James Morris in the *January 1934* edition of that paper, he is described as "an accomplished musician, being the first musical instructor of the Old Spring Gardens Mission Band. He can play almost any instrument and has been the mission choirmaster for about thirty-five years, the latter quarter of a century at the present Whitley Hall Methodist Mission of which he is a trustee."

James was described as being the first musical instructor of the Spring Gardens Mission Band and the same article records that he moved to Reading "about fifty years ago", having been born at Timsbury, Somerset in 1869. We can therefore date the start of the band to between 1884 and 1893, when it is mentioned in the Leaders' Meeting minutes as above. Mind you, James would only have been 15 in 1884 so it would seem more realistic to date the start of the band to about 1890, as it was obviously well established by 1893.

It seems from the *Souvenir of the 21st Anniversary of Whitley Hall* that: "For many years the only instrumental music for the outdoor work was that supplied by the concertinas of Messrs C H Coppuck, J Meredith and F Coppuck. Then, largely through the efforts of the Ladies' Sewing Meeting, brass instruments were bought and a Band formed. Mr James Morris was the first Bandmaster and he was succeeded by Mr W Sopp. One gentleman, Mr Barkshire, was so impressed by the influence for good that the Mission was exerting that he left a legacy of £300 for its extension. The fact is the main purpose was ever kept in view and the workers were inspired by a fervent evangelism. It was Methodism at its best."

Catherine Montague recalled that her father, Benjamin Cox, played in the Band for the first service at Whitley Hall. That same evening her mother, Gertrude, lost a baby, nine-month-old Edith May Cox, so the baby's funeral was the first to be held in the new church. The Minister, Rev Kitching, thought that the main church was too big a place for the funeral of such a small baby so he conducted it in the large schoolroom.

It is not until 1909, when the Spring Gardens Wesleyan Mission Band had transferred, along with the church, to Whitley Hall, (although, unlike the latter, it had not changed its name) that we have any more references to it in the *Minutes of the Leaders' Meeting*. On *January 20th*, we read of four of its members being chosen to serve on the band committee and of Mr Olsen proposing that a band member, who had been suspended, be reinstated.

On *July 20th*, a meeting was called especially to consider the report that the band had arranged to give sacred concerts in one of the public parks on Sunday afternoons. It had been discovered from the bandmaster and band secretary that three such concerts had been arranged "of which one had been given, one abandoned owing to unfavourable weather and one was to be given on August 15th. No Church Official had been informed." After a long and earnest discussion, it was agreed that the following letter should be sent to the band secretary:

“Having been informed by the Bandmaster and Secretary of the Spring Gardens Wesleyan Band that a sacred concert is to be given by the above Band on the afternoon of Sunday, August 15th in one of the Public Parks, the Leaders’ Meeting of July 20th, 1909 strongly deprecates such action and earnestly requests that the Band reconsider the matter, taking into serious consideration the earnest and unitedly expressed wish of the Leaders’ Meeting that this concert be not given. Also that the Leaders’ Meeting suggests that the Collecting books granted be applied for and expresses its willingness to lead the Collection. An early answer is requested.”

Mr Olsen gave notice that he would bring forward the whole matter at the next meeting, but we read that, when that occurred on *December 10th*: “Developments had made it unnecessary for Mr Olsen to carry out his intention, notice of which was given in the Minutes of the previous meeting. The matter was therefore dropped.” Later, during that same meeting, after Mr Olsen had submitted a comprehensive plan for aggressive Christian work for the winter, he proposed that “the Band be asked to march round the neighbourhood on Sunday evenings once a month calling attention to the Hall Services, instead of conducting the usual Open Air Service at 5.30 pm, and that the Church should accompany them.”

As you will read in chapter XII, which is entitled “Flushed with Success” and is about Whitley Hall’s Sunday School, many ex-scholars, including Len Rapley, A Rosa Wilson (then known as Ags Dixon) and Bob Cooper recall the Spring Gardens Band leading them to Leighton Park for the annual Sunday School treat. Bob also mentions the fact that it used to lead a parade, which included Pastor Spargo and the entire Sunday School, round the streets in the Spring Gardens area on the day of the Sunday School Anniversary.

However, not all occurrences connected with the band bring back pleasurable memories. Len Rapley recalled that the band, which often played at a short service on a Sunday prior to marching to Whitley Hall for the evening service, played “Nearer my God to Thee” on the corner of Spring Gardens and Milman Road on the Sunday following the sinking of the Titanic in 1912 when 1,500 people perished within four hours after the ship struck an iceberg just before midnight on April 14th during its inaugural voyage from Southampton to New York.

Some occurrences have been even more controversial than the issue of playing sacred concerts in public parks on Sunday afternoons. One such appeared in the *Reading Observer of May 4th, 1912* in an article entitled:

"Trades Unionist Demonstration
Coming of Age Celebration
Prominent Labour Leaders at Reading

Mr Will Thorne's Speech

"Speaking at No. 1 platform where the crowd were awaiting the arrival of Mr Will Thorne, Mr J G Butler, the prospective Socialist candidate for Reading referred to the absence of one of three bands (the Spring Gardens Wesleyan prize band) advertised to take part. A section of the religious community in the town had he said brought influence to bear on the bandsmen and it was as much as they dared do to come so they did not turn out. (Shame) But that was a religious movement as they saw it and they saw in that action another example of the great difficulty they had in trying to help the workers of the town. It was a great pity that such a blunder should have been committed as the withdrawal of the band. He wished to say that the bandsmen were willing to come (cheers) but were stopped by those in power."

G E Watkins, who joined the band in 1930 at the age of nine, had been taught to play the cornet by his father, a member of the band since 1920. At the time that Ted joined, Mr Charlie Coppuck was the conductor. He also recalled that a Mr J Hodges had previously fulfilled that role up to about 1914 when the band broke up due to the 1914 - 1918 War Years. When it reformed again in 1919, Charlie Coppuck became its conductor.

Ted's father was secretary of the band at that time, but took over as conductor about 1937 and remained so until he retired in 1975. Ted continued the family tradition as he took over as the band's conductor from his father. He recalled:

"When I joined the band we rehearsed in Whitley Hall Tuesday evenings and played concerts in the Chapel. The pastor then was J W Spargo and the Whitley Hall representatives to the band were Messrs G Morris, W Tucker and Upton. I enclose a couple of old photos from the local paper for you to see. It states the first photo was taken in 1902. As you can see they only had band hats, no uniform then, but it seems they had a uniform in the other photo of 1908. As you can see from the write up, the band played in the Tin Hut Mission Hall in Lynn Street (off Spring Gardens).

Spring Gardens Wesleyan Mission Band. 1902.

"The band broke its connections with Whitley Hall in 1933/4 and then rehearsed for a number of years at Christchurch School. I think the break up was brought about by the selling of scent cards and football tickets to obtain new uniforms and instruments, which the leaders of the chapel did not agree with.

"The band still has 30 members (a similar amount to the 1902 and 1908 ones) and do quite a number of charity concerts, but years ago we would march around the town in Hospital parades and to fetes etc. We are still self-supporting - that is one reason we don't do contesting now, because of the expense and the lack of rehearsal room. We now rehearse once a week at St George's Hall, St George's Road - we can't afford any more what with the price of instruments and music etc.

"We have quite a number of young people - boys and girls - in the band, so there is still plenty of interest in it."

The photographs mentioned by Ted had originally been sent to the *Midweek* by Raymond Searle and appeared in the *April 15th, 1986* edition of that newspaper. Raymond's father, Charles, appeared in both pictures of the Wesleyan Mission Hall Band and Raymond recalled that the Mission Hut was a tin building in Lynn Street just off Spring Gardens and was the forerunner of Whitley Hall Methodist Church. After the transfer to Whitley Hall, the mission building was in use for many years by a woodwork and pattern-making business.

The caption on the 1908 photograph stated that the band were winners of the Southern Counties Band Association challenge shield (Second Section) 1907; holders of five Association Certificates; two Berks, Bucks and Oxon Musical Festival Certificates; winners of 12 prizes (five firsts) and a set of 26 silver medals.

Starisers Drum and Bugle Corps, marching past Christ Church, while leading the Whitley Hall Sunday School on their return from the re-enactment of the Sunday School Outings to Leighton Park for the 80th Sunday School Anniversary in 1986

Chapter VII: Let us Play

Standing in the market place,
Jesus watched the children play
Where the eastern sunshine fell,
All the merry summer day:

Chorus: Praise to Jesus while we play,
Praise Him, praise Him all the day.

Verse 1 of no 598 in
The School Hymn Book of the Methodist Church
by Frederick Arthur Jackson (1867 - 1942)

The main area for play in Spring Gardens is, to this day, known as "The Tank". According to the *Reading Corporation Terrier, 1908*: "the freehold property situate in Spring Gardens and Whitley Street containing an area of one acre or thereabouts and known as the Spring Gardens Recreation Ground was formerly used as a reservoir in connection with the Waterworks undertaking of the corporation, but was appropriated for the purpose of a Public Pleasure Ground in the year 1902. A sum of £20 per annum was then paid to the Waterworks account in respect of the property together with the cottage and garden called Whitley Cottage."

Born in the year that the Tank became a Public Pleasure Ground, Len Rapley's memories of it included the playing of 'football', mostly with a tennis ball "although, occasionally, a boy would turn up with a real football and we would ask him if we could have a kick. Competitive football matches were often arranged between different roads such as Spring Gardens, Waterloo Road, Elgar Road and Mount Street. The players would finish the game covered in red brick dust!

"In the summer we would play cricket, again with an old tennis ball, any old piece of wood for the bat and the stumps were chalked out on the wall. The brick surface of the Tank was quite suitable for roller skating and some did just that.

"A number of boys practically lived in the Tank and had to be called for school, meals and bed."

H L Gilbert Heath, who was for many years a resident of Milman Road and whose grandmother, Fanny Heath, lived in Spring Gardens, commented in an article in the 15th *September, 1987* edition of the *Midweek* that 'The Tank' was: "originally a reservoir built by the Reading Waterworks Company in 1820 and enlarged in 1826. In 1852, the supply in the Spring Gardens Reservoir was used for street watering, and also by the railway. After 1877, the reservoir was used for emergency storage. It was apparently listed in Reading Directories as a reservoir as late as 1902. The part of Spring Gardens between Waterloo Road and Milman Road was in fact known as Tank Road and is so named in the Reading Directories of 1874 to 1893.

Len Cook's memories of "Football in the Tank"

"Now that many of the dwelling houses have been demolished one gets an uninterrupted view of the layout. It is used principally or was when I saw it last, as a children's playground. The inclined ramps at each end were a constant source of excitement to those with bicycles, but if you fell off your machine the brick 'ground' was scarcely kind to your knees!

"Spring Gardens Recreation Ground was a park in the fullest sense of the word and a full-time uniformed keeper was employed who lived in a cottage within the grounds at the Whitley Street end and whose name, I think, was Bowen. His son used to go to nearby Christchurch School about the same time as I was a pupil there."

Raymond Searle, who was seven years younger than Gilbert commented: "I was born in 1915 at Collis Street which I would claim as being in the Spring Gardens district and I lived there until I was married in 1940 by the Rev Priestly and then moved to Caversham.

"During my childhood, I spent many happy hours in the Tank playing football, the goalposts being chalked on the slopes each end and we never had a 'throw in' as the ball bounced off the walls and that was always part of the strategy of the Tank games. The Tank was also a short cut to the centre of Whitley Street from home via Lynn Street.

"As regards Spring Gardens, I used to traverse it several times a day to and from Palmer School. Election days were always looked forward to as we used to march up and down Spring Gardens to the polling station in Christ Church School in small gangs carrying our banners and chanting slogans for our candidate. Incidentally, you may guess that Spring Gardens district was predominantly Labour and we outnumbered our 'opponents' in any skirmishes. The Labour Party committee rooms were always held in the house of a Mr Wheeler opposite Essex Street. An evening treat was to walk up Waterloo Road to the fish and chip shop at the corner of Spring Gardens for potato fritters (5 for tuppence)."

Just six years younger than Raymond Searle, Charles Gibson too recalled games of football in the Tank, especially after school. However, as well as the chalked goal posts when the boys played, he enjoyed the time when the 'Big Boys' played. That was when the youngsters' uncles etc came home from work and the full length of the Tank was used with jackets serving for goal posts.

As well as these outdoor activities, Christ Church Institute at the top of Southampton Street catered for indoor pursuits. Back in *1909*, according to the entry in Smith's *Directory of Reading* for that year, there was a boxing club, quoits and bowls, billiards and bagatelle, a model rifle range and a bathroom on the premises. For those facilities the members paid four shillings a year or one shilling a quarter and the caretaker was Mr Daniel Hall.

Prior to that, in 1890, a member of Christ Church Institute could take part in shorthand and writing classes as well as the recreational activities. That was interpreted by Stephen Yeo in *Religion and Voluntary Organisations in Crisis* as showing that "the preoccupation of the agency was with assisting towards upward social mobility."

The land where the Institute, its car park and a tree stood at the top of Southampton Street has only, during the last decade, been used for alternative purposes when the Muir Group Housing Association built Jack Price Court there in 1992. The only sign that the Institute once stood there is the bricked-in part of the perimeter wall indicating where beer etc was taken into its cellar ready for functions such as wedding receptions.

The Methodist Church catered for the physical needs of its members and adherents just as it did for the spiritual, educational and social aspects. Over the years, the physical needs have varied, but a Whitley Wives Keep Fit group and the Mens' Recreation Club, as well as gymnastics and other physical activities for the Girls' and Boys' Brigade members were still in existence in the 1990s at Whitley Hall. Some of the younger men kept a Table Tennis Club going and the older ones were still playing billiards until the sale of the premises by the Reading & Silchester Circuit in November 1997. Earlier, the activities were probably wider ranging as people were unable to travel so easily to other parts of the town and even further afield, as they are today.

Dick Painter, who retired at the age of 70 in 1975 after spending part of his working life working in what was originally the Schoolroom of the Spring Gardens Mission, showed me the medal he won as a member of Whitley Hall's football team. It was engraved:

1923 - 4
Reading & District Institute
League Championship
W.H.F.C. R. Painter

Dick even remembered that the score when Whitley Hall Football Club won that championship was: 1 - 0. They had played Mapledurham on Coley Park Corporation football pitch. Their team colours were green and white and he knew that the team was still in existence in 1932 as he had another photograph of a friendly match with St Paul's, which was taken at that time. However, he could only recall the names of Bill Morris, Bert Upton and Bob Wells as fellow players in the photograph of the 1923-4 League Championship winning team.

Dick is pictured here as part of the 1923/4 Championship winning team

As well as the participation in games and sports, the playing of instruments and associated musical activities have played an important part in church services and weekday meetings. In addition to the Spring Gardens Band, which has already been mentioned in the previous chapter, there have always been other organisations meeting both at Spring Gardens Mission and at Whitley Hall. These have varied with regard to the concentration of religious emphasis within the activity. However, all organisations have concentrated on the whole person, rather than just the religious side. This has meant that even the choir, whose activities one would expect to be mainly religious and musical, had an Outing and a Social mentioned as annual occurrences, plus sick visiting.

We do not know when the choir was first formed, but it was definitely at Spring Gardens as James Morris was described in the *January 1934* edition of the *Methodist Times* as having been the "mission choirmaster for about 35 years, the latter quarter of a century at the present Whitley Hall Methodist Mission of which he is a trustee." Similarly, it is not known when an organ was first used to accompany the singing during services at Spring Gardens Mission, or of what type it was. However, in the *Minutes of the Leaders and Stewards Quarterly Meeting* held on *March 12th, 1900*, it is recorded that:
"A Society Tea was held January 15th, presided over by Rev W Fuller, balance from Tea 9 shillings and four & a half pence, which was voted toward the Organ Fund."

Harvest Festival at Whitley Hall showing the original American Organ in 1920

By the time the Church had transferred to the Whitley Hall premises, the music for the services was provided by an American organ, according to Rev Gordon A Durrant in the booklet he wrote for the Golden Jubilee of the Church in *1956: Retrospect and Prospect.* He also wrote: "The present organ was built by W C Vowles of Bristol and was bought from Cricklewood Parish Church in 1923 for about £320. About seven or eight years ago it was restored at a cost of £150 largely through the initiative of Mr W A Jelly who, until his retirement had been organist for 25 years; before him, Mrs Franklin and Mr Penny had held that appointment." Pictured opposite in front of the American organ is Pastor Bert Bailey with the display of produce brought for the 1920 Harvest Celebrations, held on September 20th that year:

As well as the band, there was an orchestra band, although we do not know as much about that as about the brass band. In fact, it is only in the *Minutes of the Leaders and Stewards Meeting* held on *October 2nd, 1905* that this veiled comment is made: "Recommendation from this meeting to the Superintendent that he call a Trustee Meeting as soon as possible to consider about the Orchestra Band and the hymn books for the New Chapel." Later in this book, in the table of membership of Church organisations in Chapter X, it can be seen that there were ten members of the orchestra band in 1909 and seven in 1910.

Each organisation conducted its meetings in a businesslike manner and from the minutes of those meetings, it can be seen that all points were proposed and seconded, as they are to this day. In the case of the choir, there were printed rules as on *February 24th, 1938*, it was proposed that there should be a new set of rules for choir members. A president, two vice presidents, secretary and treasurer were elected as well as a choir master (and, by 1929, an assistant choir master), six members to form the choir committee, two sick visitors, two librarians and two auditors. In *1924* - the first year for which records are now available - at the *Annual General Meeting* on *February 7th*, a choir social was to be arranged for March 13th, a choir outing for July 19th or 26th and Choir Sunday to be celebrated on Sunday and Monday, 5th and 6th October. It was also agreed at that meeting that there should be a lecture and musical items on the Monday. Choir concerts were, in fact, held until 1977 - that year, one was held on Wednesday 30th November following Choir Sunday on the 27th.

Towards the end of its continuous life, outings were still part of the life of the choir, because we read on *Friday, May 17th, 1985* under Any Other Business: "Choir Outing: Pauline Crump agreed to arrange a venue for a Dinner for Friday, 8 November."

Only the previous year, David Allaway had suggested that "instead of the usual Choir Sunday, the day should be called Music Sunday, incorporating all the music groups in the Church, such as the Whitley Hall Youth Group and a selection of the Boys' Brigade Band." At the *AGM* on *May 16th, 1986*, the decision, which had been made the previous year, that the choir should "sit together at services to assist the congregational singing and that in the autumn would meet as a music group in the homes of choir members and would learn a repertoire of music that could be introduced into special services" was ratified: "After discussion it was agreed to advise the stewards that there is now no viable choir at Whitley Hall but it had been decided to form a Fellowship of Singers to be known as The Whitley Hall Music Fellowship. This group would meet in members' homes to listen to or make music, learning a repertoire that could be used at special functions of the church."

Whitley Hall Choir with Rev Noel Richardson

Until 1985 the choir had used the seats to the side of the organ, but as numbers dwindled they decided that they would prefer to lead the singing by sitting with the congregation. However, one musical tradition remained, that being the singing of a cantata on Good Friday. For many years this had been alternately 'Olivet to Calvary' and Stainer's 'Crucifixion' sung by an augmented choir with invited soloists and the *April 20th, 1990* edition of the

Reading Chronicle reads under the heading 'Good Friday Cantata': "As is now customary, members of Whitley Hall Methodist Church marked the devotional feeling of Good Friday with a performance of J H Maunder's Sacred Cantata 'Olivet to Calvary'." In the article next to that headed 'A taste of Bohemia', we realise that Whitley Hall was to be the venue for a different style of singing on Saturday, May 12th when "the Reading Concert Singers will be presenting another in their popular series of concert versions of operas and operettas."

Other gleanings about the choir included the fact that by 1931, the age limit for the choir "was lowered to 14 years to give a wider scope for our young people". By 1944, that age limit was changed back to 15 years with the proviso that "exceptions be made in certain cases". In 1937, an electric blower was fitted to the organ. Occasionally, there are references to events happening outside the Church. As an example, the *Choir Minutes* on *May 12th, 1939* state: "It was agreed to hold our usual evening outing and Wednesday, June 28th was the date fixed . . . It was proposed by Mrs Studley and seconded by Mrs Houghton that one shilling per member be taken from the Halfpenny Fund and the balance (which might be a little more than 1*s* / 6*d* owing to Messrs Smith and Sons having taken over Mr Cox charabanc business) be paid by members."

One organisation started only just before the move to Whitley Hall was Women's Own which was formed in October, 1905. Gladys Clifford, who joined Women's Own in 1947 and became one of its registrars in 1948, still filled that role when she told me about the organisation just prior to one of its meetings on Tuesday, July 24th, 1990. At that time it followed Tuesday Lunches, so the ladies were able to socialise before the 2.15 pm meeting. In the gap between the Lunch, which started at 12.30 pm, and Women's Own, she told me that originally she was persuaded to be registrar with my great aunt Ede (Edith Emily Barnes) as "we need a young face to greet the ladies when they arrive"! Although Aunt Ede, who lived next door to my family when we resided at 232 Basingstoke Road, had been involved with Women's Own at least since 1939, when she was first mentioned as being on its committee, has long since died, Gladys, was still welcoming ladies to the weekly meetings until just before her 90th birthday. Ironically, she died on the day of the closing services at Whitley Hall on November 2nd, 1997.

However, in July, 1990, Gladys commented that, when she first took over her role, the Women's Own had 88 members but, by 1990, there were only 29 who were able to attend its meetings, plus some who are housebound. She recalled that "the big event of the year used to be Chrysanthemum Day. This was held on the first Sunday in October and all the Women's Own meetings from around the Circuit would descend on Whitley Hall, bearing their bunches of chrysanthemums. There was a Roll Call and a representative of each Women's Own group would bring their bunch of chrysanthemums to the front of the Church where the Communion area soon became filled with the flowers which were later distributed to the sick.

"For the tea on those anniversary days, there would be as many as 150 sitting down to eat. Of course, the Women's Own Anniversaries are still celebrated with a special service and a Tea but the flowers were stopped when they became very expensive."

Interestingly, just prior to the time that Gladys joined the Women's Own, the *Minutes* show that Chrysanthemum Day and the Anniversary were celebrated separately. In *1946*, the date for Chrysanthemum Day was fixed for September 24th and those for the Anniversary as Sunday, October 27th and Wednesday, October 30th.

However, on *May 27th, 1947*, the Committee decided to "amalgamate the two events as from the visitors' point of view the two big days have hitherto been too close together. So it was settled that for this year at any rate we would make one big effort which we hoped would prove successful. The Anniversary Sunday was fixed provisionally for October 12th . . . October 15th. The Wednesday afternoon combined Chrysanthemum Service and Annual Rally to commence about 3.30 pm."

The following year "it was decided to have another combined meeting as last year. Wednesday October 6th being the day agreed upon . . . . Our President had been very fortunate in securing as speaker for this gathering Mrs David Lewis (Vice-president of the Methodist Conference) an honour which we fully appreciate."

We gain some idea of what happened on such occasions from the *Minutes* where: "Chrysanthemum Service at 3.15 pm presided over (if willing) by Coun. Mrs E Langston. Wesley Bright Hour Choir to be asked to render musical items with Cumberland Rd Sisterhood as second choice. All were unanimous in their wish that Mrs W M White be asked to receive the flowers . . . . The afternoon meeting to be followed by tea after which Mr Ralph Kelly be asked to arrange a musical interlude of community hymn-singing and organ music. 7 pm was the time fixed for the evening meeting. Sister Margaret Johns to be asked to preside, or failing her, Mrs Stonham with Miss Inwards or Mrs Vine as soloist. The Speaker again being Mrs David Lewis."

Although for the Women's Own Sunday, October 10th, 1948 "the Preachers asked for being the Rev W Gowland at 11 am with a musical item by W O members. 6.30 pm Rev W M White with Miss Lovelock as soloist" did not then warrant any comment such as that accorded to Mrs David Lewis since both were presumably working in the local Circuit and indeed one was our own Minister, it is apparent to me viewing this some 43 years later that the name of Rev Bill Gowland is known to me whereas that of David Lewis is not. Unfortunately, just two months prior to my writing this section, Bill died unexpectedly on May 23rd, 1991, when in the eightieth year of his life and the 56th year of his ministry. However, by then he was also recognised as being the last former United Methodist President of Conference, 1979 (Kenneth B Garlick, *Methodist Recorder, June 13th, 1991*).

Similarly, Alan J Davies commented in Bill's *Obituary* the previous week in the *Methodist Recorder*: "So at Tilehurst, at the Albert Hall and at Wesley Church, Luton, the queues would patiently wait to talk to him . . . So it is to people, not movements or institutions, that Bill Gowland leaves his greatest legacy. The fact that he was President of Conference, founding principal of Luton Industrial College and much else in an illustrious ministry pales into insignificance beside the inspiration he gave to so many."

From the *Minutes of the Women's Own*, we can see that, as with the choir, many people were involved in its organisation. These included a president, secretary and assistant, four vice presidents, a registrar and assistant, treasurer, two pianists, a bank secretary and treasurer, two welcomers, three lookers out, two sick visitors, two auditors and ten committee members ie 33 in total on *July 31st, 1923*, the first year for which records exist.

At the following committee meeting on *September 11th, 1923*, two ladies were allocated to each of the months from October 1923 through to July, 1924 inclusive to arrange for socials. In those days, there were obviously enough interested women to form their own choir as on *January 20th, 1925* "all members with the exception of Mrs Giles agreed to start a Choir and the first practice to take place on Thursday, January 29th." It was recorded that the practice took place in the schoolroom at 3 o'clock, 14 women being present, at which Mrs Smith (the person who had offered to lead a choir) expressed her satisfaction. On *March 31st, 1925*, a rule was made that each member should pay 1/2 *d* (ie a halfpenny) weekly to choir funds for music.

It was agreed that there should be an annual outing, which, that year took the form of a char-a-banc ride to Windsor and Burnham Beeches. The previous year, there had been one to Southsea on July 1st, 1924, fare 8/3 each member (ie £0-41 in present currency) and another to Southsea in 1923 when adults were charged 8/6 and children 5/6. Members of the Women's Own were also asked by letter from the Sunday School secretary at their *April 17th, 1923 committee meeting* if they would cater for the visitors' tea at the SS treat on August 1st. Not only did they help that other church-based organisation but, at the *committee meeting* of *August 6th* that year, we read that "Mrs Dixon proposed and Mrs Fry seconded that the profit of 17/- made on the visitors tea at Sunday School Treat be given to Sunday School Fund." The yearly meeting for the election of officers, which took place on *July 28th* in *1925*, was held "in the Hall owing to workmen being in large schoolroom."

Occasionally, the minutes record the death of a very valued worker for Women's Own. As an example, at the *committee meeting* held on *January 14th, 1930*, it is written: "It was with profound regret and sorrow that a resolution was passed to put on record the loss of our dear friend and Secretary, Mrs M E Sharp, who was called to Higher Service on Saturday, December 28th, 1929. She had been twice Secretary since the beginning of the W O and was always an energetic and sympathetic worker and was greatly loved and respected." At the *committee meeting* on *September 2nd* that year "it was decided to have a framed photograph of the late Secretary (Mrs M E Sharp) to be hung in the school room with brass plate commemorating her services, the plate to be attached to the frame of the photograph."

Chapter VIII: Full to the Brim

From Thee, the overflowing spring,
Our souls shall drink a fresh supply,
While such as trust their native strength
Shall faint away, and droop, and die.

Verse 4 of no 663 in Hymns & Psalms
by Isaac Watts (1674 - 1748)

After falling to its lowest level of 47 at the beginning of 1895, the membership of Spring Gardens Mission fluctuated but reached 102 by the beginning of 1902 and its maximum of 164 by the end of 1903. Since it had been intended that the building should seat 200 and, at that stage of its history, there were more adherents than members attending most Methodist Churches, or chapels as they were so often called then, we can imagine that it was 'standing room' only at many services.

One can only guess as to why the membership increased dramatically over that period but we do know that various evangelistic services were held as for example from March 1st - 14th, 1895 under the leadership of the Evangelist, Mr Hutchinson. In the Reading Circuit generally, there was also more activity as a new century loomed, in much the same way as there has been for the start of the third Millennium. The *Minutes of the Leaders' Annual Meeting for Spring Gardens* held on 19th January, 1899 state: "A committee was formed to work the 20th Century Fund. The names of those chosen were Mr Mitchell, J Morris, Card, Pitts, Bailey in addition to the Stewards and Leaders. Mr Payn elected Secretary." According to the *List of Subscribers to the Twentieth Century Fund* kept in the safe at Oxford Road until its sale in 1996, there were 23 contributors from Spring Gardens Mission, 250 from Wesley, 212 from Oxford Road, 34 from Caversham and 9 from Tilehurst.

By May 1903, the Wesleyan Extension Scheme had been launched to raise £20,000 for four main building projects – Elm Park Hall, Caversham Heights, Tilehurst and the move of Spring Gardens Mission into the much more attractive and spacious buildings that became known as Whitley Hall.

On November 30th, 1904, the Reverend Owen Watkins (Superintendent of the Circuit) and Thomas May, along with 18 others, signed the conveyancing papers of land that on 25th and 26th March, 1807 had been released by Ebenezer Maitland to Thomas Jones and Joseph Davis. On 12th and 13th May, 1809, it had then passed to John Boult (who was described as a baker) and John Blandy, a gentleman. The latter two also bought land from Rev John Flory Howard, clerk rector of Yattendon, on 18th and 10th November, 1831.

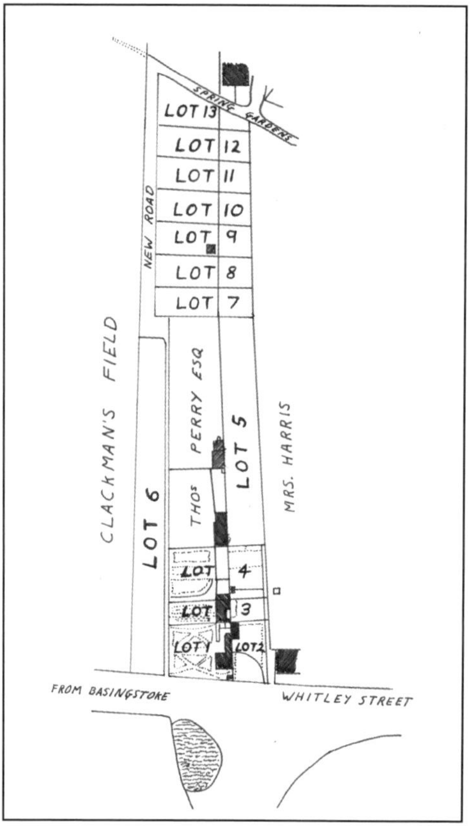

When John Boult died 'on or about 27th September, 1848', his land was auctioned by Haslams in 14 lots at the Upper Ship Inn on Thursday, April 5th, 1849 at 3 pm. It can be seen from the plan reproduced here that the land on which Whitley Hall now stands comprised Lot 1 and parts of Lots 3 and 4. At the auction, William Bishop, who was described as 'pork butcher, Whitley dairy' in Macauley's *Berkshire Directory, 1853*, bought Lot 2 - a very desirable plot of land 40 ft x 72 ft for £92; Lot 3 - a freehold dwelling house and premises 27 ft x 110 ft for £210 and Lot 5, a piece of freehold garden land 41 ft x 270 ft for £50. We are told on the *1849 auction particulars* that the house on Lot 3 contains "entrance passage, 2 sitting rooms, wash house and offices and is in the occupation of Mrs Duncombe, as yearly tenant, at an annual rent of £12."

Not all of John Boult's land was sold at that first auction so there were subsequent ones. On Friday, July 13th, 1849, again "at three o'clock in the afternoon precisely", there was a second auction at the Upper Ship Inn (now the Best Western Hotel) when “A freehold Dwelling House and garden formerly in the occupation of the late Mrs Body; a freehold Dwelling House with front and back garden late in the occupation of John Boult Esq deceased; and six plots of freehold Building Land” again came under the hammer. That time, only one plot of land seems to have been disposed of because, when a third auction was advertised as being at the Upper Ship Inn on Friday, December 7th, 1849, the description was the same as that mentioned above except that only five plots of freehold building land were offered for Peremptory Sale by Mr Haslam. Each time the dwellings and land had been offered for auction they were described as “The whole of the property is free from land-tax and most advantageously situate for building purposes.”

Lot 1 in the original auction, which had been the part where John Boult’s daughter, Olive Elizabeth Body, had lived was eventually sold on 30th January, 1850 to William Thompson Pledge, grocer of Luton. When he sold it on 26th August, 1864 to Thomas Barkshire of Silver Street, Reading, it was described as “Conveyance of Rose Cottage, Whitley Street for £320”. The Barkshires continued to call 112, Whitley Street, Rose Cottage - quite an aptly-named residence for a seed grower, as Thomas Barkshire was. However, according to the *street directory of 1895*, the name seems by then to have changed to Oakhurst.

Although 6 Boults Walk, once part of Lot 4 and previously in the occupation of Thomas Griffith Boult, is only mentioned as having a name in the *1859 street directory* when it was given as Laurel Cottage, under item 6 of the *Deeds* deposited by H F Andrews of Messrs Dennis Berry & Co in March 1963 in the Shire Hall Record Office Archives, it is described as “Conveyance of the Laurels, Boults Walk, Reading, Berks.”

By the time of the *street directory of 1865*, Mr William Allport was named as the householder but, according to the Deeds, it was not until December 28th, 1875 that he actually bought the property from Catherine Haslam, Dryland Haslam and Virgoe Buckland. We can recognise this as being part of Lot 4 at the 1849 auction, in that it has a frontage towards the private road of 61ft 6ins but the depth is only 64ft in contrast to the 107ft mentioned under Lot 4 where the house was described as containing an entrance passage, two sitting rooms, cellar, wash-house and offices, two bedrooms and two attics.

Thus it can be seen that Whitley Hall was built on the sites of both Rose Cottage and Laurel Cottage, giving added meaning to this piece of research as my first name, Daphne, means Laurel, and my mother's first name was Rose. Amazingly, I discovered that the Children's Corner, which was erected in memory of my mother (who died on August 7th, 1972), in fact stood on part of the site where Rose Cottage once stood and that Whitley Hall's Small Schoolroom, in which I taught the younger members of the Sunday School for almost 30 years, is where Laurel Cottage stood - coincidences I would probably never have known about had I not decided to carry out this research.

◄ Daphne, with Rev E Donald Mason at the dedication of Whitley Hall's Children's Corner, July 1973, in memory of her mother, Rose Barnes.

According to Rev Gordon Durrant in *Retrospect and Prospect*, 4 Boult's Walk and its 1,890 square feet was purchased on 30th November, 1904 for £250. "On February 14 the next year they purchased No. 6, Boults Walk with an additional 6,000 square feet for £515" and, thirteen days later, 112 Whitley Street, which gave a frontage of 75 feet, for £550. On 12th July, 1905, seven foundation stones were laid, the first by Rev Owen Watkins, who conducted the ceremony and who also laid £20 on the stone.

However, it is not until October 2nd, 1905 that there is any mention of the New Chapel in the *Minutes of the Leaders' and Stewards' Meeting for Spring Gardens* when the following entry appears: "Recommendation from this meeting to the Superintendent that he call a Trustee Meeting as soon as possible to consider about the Orchestra Band and the hymn books for the New Chapel." In the summary of the next *Leaders' and Stewards' Meeting* held on *January 8th, 1906*, it was stated: "Also the possibility of holding a Covenant Service first Sunday in the New Hall at 8.30 in the morning."

The name 'Whitley Hall' does not seem to have been used until later that month when in the *Minutes* of the next Meeting on *January 22nd, 1906*, we read: "Proposed by Mr Coppuck, seconded by Mr Franklin that a P S A be formed at Whitley Hall to be started on the first Sunday of the opening. Proposed that sanction of the Trustees be obtained." At that same meeting, it was proposed that a Covenant Service be held on March 18th at 8.30 in the morning - the first Sunday after the opening of the Hall - "and that Tickets of Membership be shown on admittance, also any Believer wishing to take part in the service may do so, by applying to the Leader for a ticket." Nowadays, although tickets of membership are given to Pastoral Leaders at the annual Covenant service (held now in January at the start of the New Year) for distribution to members of their Classes, I have never had to show one during my 40 year's membership of the Methodist Church.

The Opening Ceremony of Whitley Hall warranted a three column spread in the *Saturday, March 17th, 1906* edition of the *Reading Standard.* This included a pen drawing of the facade and made the comment that: "Standing as it does on some of the highest ground in the borough, Whitley Hall is an attractive building in all senses. It appeals to the eye in external appearance, and internally the visitor is impressed with the capacity of its accommodation, its quiet, but effective decoration, and its air of comfort with utility. It is in marked contrast to the places which have been the home of the Wesleyans in Spring Gardens for the 50 years since the work commenced, places which have been unostentatious, almost obscure, but where, nevertheless, service has been rendered with earnestness and devotion. But the new position and the increased accommodation of the building will be in perfect accord with the spirit of the times (which calls for strenuousness even in Church life) and with the growth of the population and the need in the neighbourhood which it is intended to serve. The hall boldly faces the main road, and, having thus invited the passer-by is capable of entertaining him within." That article was headed:

"Opening of Whitley Hall
Another Step towards the Completion of the Wesleyan Extension Scheme.
Another generous offer by Mr George Gilligan.
Nearly £17,000 now raised."

The report placed Whitley Hall in the context of the Wesleyan Extension Scheme, which commenced in May, 1903 in the Reading Circuit. It was the third of five phases to be completed, the previous two being Tilehurst and Elm Park Hall (which became the home of West Reading Methodist and is now Emmanuel Methodist after that church and Oxford Road Methodist combined in 1996) and the two still in contemplation at that stage being those in 'Cholmely - road and Caversham'.

An interesting feature of the opening ceremony for today's readers is that it took place on a Wednesday afternoon - March 14th - and was naturally followed by a tea and evening meeting. Presumably, this was partly because, at that time, shops practised half-day closing on Wednesdays as the only other time shopkeepers were not expected to work was Sunday.

I can remember being a bridesmaid at Whitley Hall on a Wednesday afternoon at my Uncle Wilf's wedding on July 22nd, 1953 when he, Wilfred Barnes (my father's younger brother) married Ismay Beasley, so, half a century later, the custom was still widely upheld. In the photograph taken outside Whitley Hall, I am standing next to the bridegroom with my paternal grandparents behind.

My brother, Alan, is next to the other bridesmaid with our parents behind her.

As we have seen, the members of Spring Gardens Mission were in the habit of holding a Wednesday evening service, either weekly or fortnightly, and in fact they continued that practice when they transferred to Whitley Hall. Even after the cessation of the regular Wednesday evening meetings, it was still the custom to have a Wednesday afternoon and evening meeting to celebrate the Church Anniversary until 1980. The following year, which was Whitley

Hall's 75th, Anniversary in that building, I had recorded in my *diary* for *Wednesday, March 18th, 1981:* "Anniversary tea at 5.30 pm. Four rows of chairs had been arranged at the tables (these would have been trestle tables which stretched the length of the Large Schoolroom) but only two were filled. It was suggested that the reason for this was that it was the first year there had not been an afternoon service." By 1982, the tradition of an anniversary tea on the Sunday afternoon was established and, on March 14th that year, it cost each person 40p!

We are told that the opening ceremony, like that of the foundation stone laying, was favoured "with splendid weather, bright sunshine prevailing during the brief open-air proceedings. The door was formally opened by Mrs Ann Davis (whose husband, James, had built Wesley Manse in 1899) in the presence of a large gathering which included the architect, Mr W Roland Howell, ARIBA; the builder, Mr Robert Curtis; Rev F L Wiseman of Birmingham and Rev Grainger Hargreaves of Oxford as well as local clergy and representatives of the Wesleyan Methodist societies in the circuit.

"The ceremony opened with the singing of the hymn 'All people that on earth do dwell' and prayer by the Rev J Edward Peel. Mr Howell then presented to Mrs Davis a silver-gilt key, with which to unlock the main outer door. In doing so, he said the building before them was the latest offspring of the Wesleyan Extension Scheme. It had been his privilege to act as its architect, and he wished to take that opportunity of saying that the committee, while exercising due and necessary restraint, had been very kind and courteous to him throughout. They had allowed him certain latitude in arranging the building, which had been erected not necessarily on the strict lines of precedent but with the object of making it suitable for the work for which it was intended. He paid a tribute to the very satisfactory way in which Mr Curtis and his foreman (Mr Holder) had built the place, with no desire to make a large profit from it. (Hear, hear.) He asked Mrs Davis' acceptance of the key,

> in the first place to open the door of a building which he hoped would be a blessing to that part of Reading, and,
>
> secondly, as a souvenir of an occasion which he hoped she would long be spared to remember as a happy one.

“Mrs Davis then unlocked the door and, standing just inside the entrance and vestibule, said she was glad the time had passed when a plain square building in a back street was considered good enough for God’s House. Now they selected the choicest sites and sought out the most eminent architects in order that their churches and halls might be of the best and most beautiful. She asked them to look at that building, unique in its design, majestic in its proportion, and ornate in its detail, and said that she opened the door and threw it wide not only for Methodists but for that great class designated in the ‘Whosoever’. (Hear, hear). It was with very great pleasure and some amount of pride that she performed that duty that afternoon. For whosoever entered that door there was a welcome and hope.

“After the superintendent minister, Rev J G Warrington, had expressed his gratefulness that ‘one of our own’ had performed the duty of declaring the hall open and Mr Davis had responded on behalf of his wife, the hall was then thrown open and speedily filled for the first time. As soon as a photograph of the scene had been taken, Rev Warrington read the declaration of the registration of the building for public worship. Then followed a religious service and a public tea.”

Apparently, the hall was again crowded for the public meeting that followed the tea. This time the gathering was presided over by one of the pioneers of the Wesleyan Home Missions (Mr Thomas Walker of Bolton), the singing was led by the Spring Gardens Band, a harmonium, and a choir, and inspiring addresses were delivered by the Rev F L Wiseman, BA (of the Birmingham Mission), the Rev Grainger Hargreaves (of Oxford), and others.

The Rev F L Wiseman came early in the programme to enable him to return home that evening. He began by quoting the words of a famous statesman: “We are not down-hearted”. He went on to say that, although many men and women in middle life in the present generation were of “noble ideal but sardonic spirit”, aspiring only to getting a motor car or joining a golf club, the Methodists of Reading had the source of power as well as the ideal. As a result, they were building halls “in the last year or so, and that did not look as if they believed Christianity was played out. People had come to their assistance and £15,000 had already been paid out of the £20,000 required. They were announcing to Reading, and indeed to all England that they were still confident the battle could be won, and that the Church of Christ could secure the victory again in these decades as it had done in former days (Hear, hear). They were by no means discouraged. On the contrary they were enheartened, and those halls had multiplied all over the land during the last 15 or 20 years. There was not one that had not been filled Sunday after Sunday by the people who had flocked to hear of the Gospel, and he thought the success of other places would be repeated in the building in which they were assembled (Applause)".

Mr Thomas May then gave the treasurer's statement, detailing that the estimated cost of the hall, inclusive of heating, lighting, boundary fences, etc. was £4,729, which together with the cost of the site, £1,500, made a total of about £6,500. Naturally, Mr May also mentioned the gifts that had been made, including £6 14*s* from the Wesley Guild, being the profit on the stone-laying tea and £21 from that day's tea. They had spent £15,198 9*s* 10*d*, and, at the stone-laying, £2,250 was required to open the hall free of debt. Since then, this had been reduced to £1,770 by further gifts and, with the £800 coming from the Manchester Committee, they had less than £1,000 to raise to clear the debt, and he urged them to do that at the meeting.

The Chairman said that in Reading "a new departure had been made in the history of Wesleyan Home Missions for instead of building those halls outside the circuit they were building their's inside it. The other halls had been separated and carried on apart from the circuit, partly because of the opposition which had obtained in some places and partly to give those in charge a freer hand. They were very much interested in the Reading movement, and prayed that God's spirit would be laid upon them, and that the halls they were building for the people would be wonderful successes.

"The chapels did not invite outsiders. There was no provision for them. They were not heartily welcomed, and the pews were reserved for and were the preserve of the regular worshippers. They must therefore build places to which the people could come freely, where they would be heartily welcomed, and where every seat would be entirely free. The working classes were not opposed to the Gospel, but went in thousands to those halls to hear it preached. A debt, he continued, on a hall like that was an encumbrance, as there was no revenue to be gained from pew rents; and he therefore hoped they would speedily discharge all liabilities."

After congratulating the friends of the Reading Circuit, Rev Grainger Hargreaves of Oxford mentioned that he thought "Methodism was gradually solving the great problems that were facing the Christian Church and adapting herself to the changed and changing conditions to get the people within sound of the Gospel. While he denied that they were not so successful in their work as their fore-fathers were, he thought it necessary they should understand present-day conditions and contrast them with those of a century ago. He thought that the wonderful success of the 18th century was achieved in 4 ways

1. the dominant note of their preaching was the moral government of the universe and the seriousness of sin and the responsibility of man. The emphasis had now changed to the fatherhood of God, and while that was important, an equilibrium of truth needed to be restored
2. their fathers believed in a spiritual change at conversion of which the individual himself was conscious and which was evident to all around whereas so often they were satisfied with respectability rather than regeneration, and good works rather than with grace in the heart
3. their fathers believed in the power of prayer
4. their fathers believed in fellowship and communion with their fellow Christians."

Mr George Gilligan, JP, in the course of an impressive address, pleaded for greater consecration and loyalty to Christ, and offered to add £1,000 to the sum they could raise by June 30th if they did their very utmost and tried to clear off the whole debt by that time. This splendid offer was the outstanding feature of a most enthusiastic meeting especially since Mr Gilligan had already given £2,000 while his late father had contributed another £1,000 to the Wesleyan Extension Scheme.

So what was this new hall like? The article, as well as saying that the buildings were specially designed to meet the requirements of the religious works proposed to be carried on, described the premises in detail:

"The large hall measures 51ft by 68ft on the ground floor, but on the gallery level the length is increased to 78ft. It has an open pitch-pine roof, which has been successfully designed to aid the acoustic properties of the hall. The decorative finishings of the walls are not yet completed, but the light woodwork and the ample windows (glazed with tinted glass in leads) already gives a bright and cheerful appearance. The hall is approached from the front through a spacious vestibule with two stone staircases leading to the gallery; a third staircase (also of stone) gives access to the other end of the gallery. The body of the hall is furnished with chairs, and the gallery with tip-up seats, the whole giving accommodation for nearly 900 persons.

"Behind the hall is a large schoolroom measuring 35ft 6in by 53ft. It is faced internally with the new sand lime bricks recently introduced into this country by Messrs S and E Collier. These bricks give a very bright appearance to the room. The other accommodations comprise an infants' room, minister's vestry, various classrooms, kitchens and the usual sanitary accommodation. The main hall and approaches are lighted by electricity, and the schoolroom block by incandescent gas.

Opening of Whitley Hall on March 14, 1906

"The street front is of a somewhat unusual character, and has been designed with the idea of giving a feeling of breadth and simplicity. The main feature is the handsome tracery window, with a bold curved cornice above it. This prominent curved line - 'the outline of beauty' - is happily contrasted by the straight termination of the main parapet. The stained glass was from the studio of Messrs Swaine, Bourne & Sons, of Birmingham; the electric lighting and heating works have been carried out by Messrs Callas, Sons & May and the wrought ironwork is by Mr Girdler of Vastern-road."

Chapter IX: Still Waters run Deep

Not for ever by still waters
Would we idly rest and stay;
But would smite the living fountains
From the rocks along our way.

Verse 3 of no 436 in Hymns & Psalms
by Love Maria Willis (1824 - 1908)

And what was the Spring Gardens area like during the early years of the changeover to Whitley Hall? Len Rapley described the memories of his childhood years there from about 1909 until 1913:

"The majority of houses were rented from large property owners, and people could move freely from one to another as there were many empty and available. I understood that the reason my family moved from Highgrove Street to Spring Gardens was that the rent was six pence (6d) a week less there. People would sit in their front gardens during the summer months, so there was always someone around to chat.

"The road surface was of gravel, and 'gravel rashes' were commonplace on children's knees and arms as a result of their falling in the road whilst playing, often with iron or wooden hoops. Peat spread in front of a house to quieten the noise of passing vehicles indicated that there was someone seriously ill in there. The water-cart was a frequent visitor during hot dry weather as the gravel needed to be prevented from filling the atmosphere with dust - the seasons were definitely more predictable in those days.

"Several milkmen - the milk was ladled from can to jug then – and also bakers and greengrocers called most days. Of those, the milkman, Mr Hamblin, had a son, Frank, who was an officer in the 1st Reading Boys Brigade. It was his 'call-up' that hastened the disbanding of the Company for the duration of the 1914 - 1918 War. Another roundsman with Whitley Hall connections was Mr Honey, the greengrocer, who with his horse and cart conveyed children from the Primary Department of the Sunday School to and from Leighton Park for the annual treat. Mr Pounds, did similar with his horse and van, which were normally used to carry out most of the removals in the area. His son, Maurice, who later carried on the business, was in the Chapel Choir.

"There was a greengrocer, Mr Williams, at the lower end of the road between Tiddley Hill (an alley-way into Whitley Street) and Southampton Street. Vegetables could be relied on to be fresh as they were mainly grown at his nursery in nearby Waterloo Road. He had a son we knew at George Palmer as 'Squeaker'.

"On the opposite side of the road toward Waterloo Road was a Confectionery shop owned by a Mr Young. He was particularly noted for his hot faggots and peas, also loose pickles. On the corner of Lynn Street was another shop selling mainly confectionery, the owner being a lady whose name I have forgotten, although I lived next door! Memories here are of 'Milky Chew-Chew' Toffee, which was very light and you could get a large amount for a penny. In addition, there was 'Sharp's Creamy Toffee' - plain or walnuts - which was in trays and was broken up with a little hammer. It was also possible to obtain a bag of 'waste' (sweets etc) for a half-penny. There was another general shop on the left corner of Essex Street, and, opposite that, was Mrs Mander's Grocery Shop where we could buy butter, cheese, eggs etc. Being the eldest of three boys, I often did the errands.

"On the other side of Spring Gardens was Annie Greenaway's Greengrocer's Shop where us children would buy Locust Beans and Tiger Nuts. A black cat could often be seen curled up in the window in the middle of a pile of the Locust Beans. On the same side, towards Milman Road, was Rumble's Shop and Dairy. The shop was run by two sisters and it was from there that we obtained our milk."

The fact that Len's interests in those days centred round the Methodist Church can possibly be most forcibly seen in the fact that, although he could remember that there were four public houses in the area, he could only recall the name of one of them, viz 'The Royal William' and the landlord of the one on the corner of Waterloo Road whose name was Mr Froude.

I don't suppose the youngsters of today will be able to recall the names of their local Bobby when they are in their eighties or nineties - we did not even have one when I was a child! However, Len could not only recall the Patrol Policeman, PC Barber, but also the fact that there were two policemen living in the road, PC 'Jumbo' Allen (whose grandson, Derek Allen, is still a member of Whitley Methodist Church) and PC Gillings. He especially remembered that PC Barber had the habit of appearing round a corner just as a tennis ball was being kicked in the road and wonders how many he collected!

Dick Painter also remembered an encounter with PC Barber on his return from bird nesting in the Northcourt Avenue area. He had almost reached home when he encountered the officer who demanded to see what he had in his pockets. It was, in fact, a rabbit which Dick had removed from a snare in a garden in Northcourt Avenue.

"Well, well! This needs a bit of looking into!" was PC Barber's response to such a statement and Dick had to accompany him to the house where a man verified his story. As a result, Dick was let off with a warning, but he didn't know what happened to the rabbit - imagined that it ended up as a free meal for PC Barber!

Youngsters could certainly be expected to be reprimanded by their elders more in those days. My father, Ted Barnes, recalled being given a good telling off when, as a teenager full of the joys of spring, he jumped off a tram before it had fully stopped. In a letter, he sent to the local press, he wrote:

"I shall never forget my first long trouser suit – a light grey one. While returning from shopping in town sporting this new outfit, I decided to jump off the tram as it slowed down outside the Wellington Arms in Whitley Street to go from the single line to the double instead of waiting until it reached the actual stopping place at Whitley Pump.

As I jumped, I not only lost my footing, but split my trousers the whole length of the inside seam. On top of this, the conductor gave me a good dressing down, and I had to sit on the pump seats until it got dark before venturing to walk the rest of the way home. Fortunately for me, the streets weren't very well lit in those days – about 1922 or 1923 – and I reached home in Long Barn Lane without too many blushes!"

Whitley Pump

Bob Cooper's memories of the shops in Whitley Street from about 1927 to 1932, when he would have been five to ten years of age, appeared in the *January/February 1992* edition of *Newslink* under the heading 'Bobbing about in Whitley Street' and are as follows:

"(Starting from the southern end on the eastern side)

Syklemore	-	Greengrocery and fruiterers
Jelly's Stores	-	Grocery & provisions(formerly World Stores)

(It will be recalled that Mr Jelly was Whitley Hall's organist for a number of years)

Dunlops	-	Corn and seed merchant
Bennetts	-	Confectioners
Miss Allwood	-	Newsagent, confectionery etc.
Fletchers	-	Butchers
Collins	-	Drapery etc.

Dearlove - Greengrocery and fruiterer

At this point there were one or two private houses, complete with front gardens, railing and gates (Reference to the dated plaques in the pavement will confirm the year that these houses were made into shops if the plaques still exist).

[Editorial comment: I found such a plaque bearing the details "Reading Corporation 1930" near the pedestrian crossing in January 2001]

The next shop I recall at this point is:

Ruddles Gents outfitter

Possibly another private house at this point

Owens	-	Portrait photographers
Eighteen & Cox	-	Butcher and fishmongers
Louis Rogers	-	Provisions, pork butchers, cooked meats
Goodys	-	Watchmaker and jeweller

(with the clock in the window proclaiming Greenwich Mean Time)

Jellys Stores	-	Grocery etc.
Miss Bance	-	Confectionery etc.
Stamps	-	Greengrocer and fruiterer
Coopers	-	Chemist and pharmacist
Home & Colonial	-	Grocery and provisions
Pounds	-	Furniture and removers
Cripps	-	Bakers and sub Post Office
Crockers	-	Dairy
Waldron	-	Butcher and greengrocery
Mence Smith	-	Hardware and oil merchant
Potters	-	Newsagent and Stationers
Co-operative Stores	-	Grocery and provisions

At this point there was a tobacconist/confectioner with a hairdressing salon at the rear of the premises, the name escapes me but I do recall that there was a carbonated drinks dispenser on the counter.

Here was a general store	-	name not known
Pottingers	-	Ladies and Gents hairdresser

[Editorial note: The interior of Pottingers can now be found in Blake's Lock Museum, Gas Works Road, Reading]

The Reading and Caversham Laundry, known then, I think, as the Snowflake.

"On the western side of Whitley Street next to Whitley Hall was a Dairy, where I was sent on many occasions, jug in hand, for a pint of milk. After the row of cottages came Glaziers, Fishmongers and Fried Fish. On the corner of

Essex Street was Merritts - Cycles, Repairs and Oil Merchant. At the Southampton Street end there was Emmitts - hairdresser and further down Mr Cole - Shoe Repairer and Mr King - Radios. Their shop was up several steps. Next came Shackleford's Bottled Mineral Water Works and then the Tea and Coffee Stall. Just round the corner was Williams - Fruiterer and Greengrocer. Mr Williams Jnr was, of course, a familiar figure in the area, doing his rounds with his horse and cart, selling his wares from door to door. In Spring Gardens there were a number of General Stores and front room shops, perhaps the most noteworthy being that of the Misses Rumble who stocked everything from sweets to milk and vegetables to hardware.

Photograph taken in April 2000 of the replica of the original Whitley Pump, which was installed in the centre of the roundabout during May, 1999

"It was a sad time for all when the Whitley Pump was demolished and the triangle opposite Whitley Hall disappeared to make way for the roundabout.

The old Whitley Pump was patronised by many of the working horses in those days. The triangle itself with its several lime trees surrounded by circular, metal slatted seats was a very popular meeting point for many of the aged locals, and I recall it was used for many public meetings, particularly at election times.

"In those days there were no restrictions for traffic which could pass on any side of the triangle. This mattered little because the small amount of cars on the road meant there was virtually no likelihood of a collision occurring. The trams that used to terminate at Whitley Pump had, of course, given way several years earlier to the trolley buses. I recall that, during the School Summer Holidays, in the days of the tram, for one old penny I could travel to Caversham Bridge and back. There were also the days when, as pupils of George Palmer School, we were marched up Basingstoke Road to join several waiting trams to be transported to the town to see Safety First films at the Central Cinema - one of the highlights of the year. It would be good to return to the days when petrol exhaust was rare and diesel fumes unknown.

"The standard of service offered by shopkeepers and traders of those days bears no comparison to those of the post-war era. Bread and vegetables were brought to one's door and many milkmen made two deliveries each day. There were many other visitors who were frequently seen on the roads in those days - the muffin man with his bell; the rag and bone man who would gladly accept anything from a jam jar to a rabbit skin; the knife and scissor grinder; the barrel organ player, complete with monkey; the man who came round each week with his ladder and wound the clocks in the street gas lamps and renewed the mantles; the horse-drawn water tank cleaning out and flushing the drains; the Spanish onion seller with his cycle laden with bunches of onions; the errand boys on their cycles making deliveries; the Walls and Eldorado icecream salesmen on their tricycles; and horses and carts delivering items from some of the larger shops.

"I wonder how many can recall the estate and park land that used to exist where Bourne Avenue and Clent Road now stands, at the end of which there was a fence where deer could regularly be seen. Opposite where the Telephone Exchange now stands, there was a high brick and flint wall surrounding the park. At the side of the row of houses from the corner of Swainstone Road there was a lodge and large gates at the entrance of the drive leading to the house.

"There are many memories that I can still vividly recall (in October 1991): the time when Poultons Brick Works in Elgar Road was burnt out and, watching it, with many others, from the wall at the end of Milman Road; seeing one of the German passenger-carrying airships fly over (either the Graf Zeppelin or the Hindenburg); watching the steam rollers when the roads were resurfaced; and further afield - my first visit to the Savoy Cinema on the corner of Buckland Road and Basingstoke Road just after its opening; the wonderful aroma of strawberries when the Co-op Jam Factory was making jam; the slums of Silver Street and Coley; the excitement of going to the junction of London Road and London Street to see the first set of traffic lights working; and many more.

"How near was Whitley Hall in those days to the open country when Northumberland Avenue ended with a fence where Hexham Road now is and Home Farm was on the opposite side of the road and the whole of the Whitley estate was nothing but fields. From that point in Northumberland Avenue there was a track to Whitley Wood Road which was quite a popular walk. On the way just one house was passed and it had a model replica of Eddystone Lighthouse in the garden. Access to Cressingham Road was from Northcourt Avenue and ended with a fence at the brow of the hill (now Birdhill Avenue). The Public Houses in Basingstoke Road: The Four Horseshoes (now Mongolian Barbeque), The World Turned Upside Down (now a Harvester) and The Grenadier (now The Post House Hotel) were little more than country cottages until they were rebuilt, and the Whitley Wood single decker bus used to terminate at The Grenadier.

"Although my memory is rapidly approaching its 'sell by date', I could still go on for many hours recalling sad and happy memories of my childhood and youth in the Whitley area. I shall always recall them as the GOOD OLD BAD DAYS and the HAPPIEST TIME OF MY LIFE."

Chapter X: Tributaries

Where streams of living water flow
My ransomed soul he leadeth,
And where the verdant pastures grow,
With food celestial feedeth.

Verse 2 of no 69 in Hymns & Psalms
by Henry Williams Baker (1821 - 77)

As well as the church services and weekday evening meetings of a religious nature, Sunday School and the band, other organisations have always met at both Spring Gardens Mission and at Whitley Hall. These have varied with regard to the degree of concentration of religious emphasis within the activity. However, all organisations have concentrated on the whole person, rather than just the religious side. This has meant that even the choir, whose activities one would expect to be mainly religious, has an outing and a social mentioned as an annual occurrence, plus sick visitors.

One of the organisations which had not been in existence at Spring Gardens Mission was the PSA. At a *Leaders and Stewards Meeting* held on *January 22nd, 1906*, it was proposed (after four members had been elected on the 8th to enquire into the working of a PSA), that a PSA should be formed at Whitley Hall starting on the first Sunday after the Opening. At that same meeting it was proposed that a Committee of 18 be formed, consisting of 12 men and 6 women, nine being elected at the Leaders' Meeting and nine elected annually from the General meeting. It was also proposed that the Minister in charge of the Hall should be the President. The representatives chosen by the Leaders' Meeting were the Messrs Harris, Payn, Coppuck, Simpson, G Coppuck and G Morris; and Mesdames Franklin, Heath and Herring. It was also decided that a public meeting should be called after the Home Missionary Evening on February 5th to elect the other nine.

To those who, like me, had not heard the term 'PSA' before, it was very baffling to come across references to it in *Street Directories* with no indication as to what the initials might mean. I even discovered that a former inhabitant of 12 Rowley Road - my home while writing this section - John

Rabson, who later became Mayor of Reading in 1922, was secretary of 'The Reading PSA Society', which was formed by Rev R H Sewell in February, 1892. In that same article in Smith's *Directory of Reading, 1909*, appearing under the heading *Religious and Benevolent Societies*, it was stated that the Reading PSA Society had grown from 80 to over 600 members in the meantime.

Its object was described as being "to provide a religious service of a bright and attractive character for those who, although outside all the Churches yet realise that 'man does not live by bread alone'. It is non-political and unsectarian. It has a book fund in connection with which several thousand volumes have already been distributed. Its meetings are held in Broad Street Chapel (now ironically Waterstones Bookshop) every Sunday afternoon from 3.30 to 4.30 pm. Their duration is brief, their character bright and their spirit brotherly."

Although the Reading PSA members were all men over 17 years of age, the Oxford Road PSA, which may well have been the first local PSA in a Methodist Chapel when it was founded in January 1895, was open to both sexes. It would seem that Whitley Hall followed that pattern as Sylvia Main recalled for the *September/October 1989* edition of *Newslink* after I had discovered from her that the initials PSA stood for 'Pleasant Sunday Afternoon':

"As a little girl of about five to six years, my grandmother would take me of a Sunday afternoon (at 2.45 pm) to PSA. This was a service very much like Women's Own, although I believe men attended, and I do so well remember that, when the Speaker got up to speak, my grandmother would cover me in her cape (as she wore a cape and bonnet) and I would have a little nap until the Speaker finished. The meeting was held in No. 4 vestry (which later became known as the Beginners' Room and is now the Billiards Room) and I remember that it was in some way partitioned off and made into two separate rooms. Much later, as a teenager, I do remember the same vestry being enlarged and made as it is today."

As well as the PSA, we gain some indication of the other organisations that were in existence in the early days at Whitley Hall from a *Leaders and*

Stewards Meeting held on *Wednesday, January 9th, 1907*. That was the meeting where the formation of the Whitley Hall Benevolent Fund was first mooted. In addition to the suggestion that the Minister in charge should be president and the two Society Stewards vice presidents and ex-officio members of committee, the composition of the committee tells us which organisations were in operation at the time as it was decided that there should be two representatives from each of the following: Bible Class, PSA, Sewing Meeting, Brotherhood, Women's Own, Sunday School and Leaders' Meeting.

Almost three years after the formation of the PSA, permission was granted for a Boys' Life Brigade Company to hold its inaugural meeting on January 30th, 1909 in the schoolrooms. During the previous July there had been 'long, friendly' discussions among the Management Committee members about the formation of a Boys' Brigade Company.

Eventually the following resolution was passed: "That this meeting recognising the Military Spirit which the Boys' Brigade fosters refuses to sanction such a Brigade believing, as they do, that Militaryism is against the principles of Christ's teaching. But at the same time sanctioning a Boys' Life Brigade whose Teaching and Principles is the saving of Life." An amendment: "That a Boys' Brigade be started if the opportunity presents itself" and the fact that the proposition, for which the voting was by ballot, was only carried by five votes to four indicates how controversial this issue was at the time.

The annual membership returns for Organisations connected with Whitley Hall on February 2nd, 1909; March 5th, 1910 and February 7th, 1911 lists the Boys' life Brigade along with 13 other such Organisations, as shown on the next page.

From the table, it can be seen that the Band of Hope was almost as popular an activity as PSA. In fact, by the time of the *1909* Smith's *Directory of Reading*, it was mentioned in the description of Whitley Hall under the Wesleyan Methodists title as:

"Services - Sunday 11am, 6.30 pm, PSA 3 pm, Wednesday 8 pm,
Temperance Meeting, Saturday 8 pm. Pastor A F Olsen."

	1909	1910	1911
Sunday School	41T & 395S	35T, 15JT & 394S	32T, 12JT & 328S
Band of Hope	57	150	112
PSA	300	200	
Women's Own	98	73	81
Brass Band		21	27
Choir	27	32	34
Orchestra Band	10	7	
Women's Slate Club	34	55	62
Men's Slate Club	69	81	
Benevolent Fund		5	
Sick Fund	51- 9 month	54	50
Wesley Guild	107-3 month	77	
Boys' Life Brigade	55B & 6 O	45 B & 6 O	20 B & 3 O
Sewing Meeting			

Key:
Sunday School: T = Teachers; JT = Junior Teachers; S = Scholars
Boys' Life Brigade: B = Boys; O = Officers.

One of those weekly 'Band of Hope' Temperance meetings obviously had a profound effect on one of the youngsters present as Len Rapley recalled, on *September 24th, 1990*, that a Mr Drake put a raw piece of meat into a test tube of alcohol. By the time he dropped it onto the platform the following week, it was as hard as stone - a salutary lesson as to how alcohol can affect one's own internal organs. Naturally, many of the Band of Hope members 'signed the pledge' that they would refrain from strong drink and the youngsters were encouraged to join the Little White Ribbonners - Len passed his badge on to me during the 80th celebrations of Whitley Hall Sunday School in 1986. He commented that Temperance organisations were very important at Whitley Hall while he worshipped there, possibly because strong drink was recognised as a great social evil then in much the same way as drugs are regarded today. He remembered there being activities most days at Whitley Hall and summed up with the comment:

"In fact we pretty well lived there - it was our life - there was nothing else!"

As well as the Band of Hope, the Whitley branch of a Temperance Benefit Society called the Independent Order of Rechabites, Livesey Tent met every fourth Friday at Whitley Hall. According to Smith's *Directory of 1909*, the secretary then was Mr A Webb of 35 Edgehill Street.

During my childhood and teenage years in the 1950s and 1960s, Temperance activities still figured prominently at Whitley Hall. Members of both Junior Christian Endeavour and the Girls' Life Brigade were encouraged to sit the temperance examinations - not that we needed much persuading when we realised that the value of the book prizes awarded for those examinations were higher than for the scripture examination or for Sunday School attendance! Sue Gregory and I went on a week's holiday at Matlock, Derbyshire with the Reading Temperance Society, when Fred Jackman was its leader, and I can also remember another member of the Harmony Gospel Group, Veronica Southey, being crowned Temperance Queen one year.

As can be seen from the table, the churches in those days even helped people in the management of their financial affairs. Sylvia Main recalled in 1989 that "Mr and Mrs Benjamin Cox (the parents of a present-day member of Whitley Hall, Catherine Montague) used to run a Slate Club and people from all round as well as Church members came to No. 1 Vestry on Friday evenings to pay their subscription. It was well patronised and many were sorry when it finished."

Obviously, a similar arrangement was still in operation in 1928 because, on the *programme* for the Rainbow Bazaar, which can be seen on the following page, it was mentioned that Thrift card holders would receive the amounts subscribed, in money tokens only, on the afternoons of the Bazaar.

From this *Official Guide and Quotation Booklet*, we can see that the following organisations were still in existence at Whitley Hall as they each ran Stalls for that event: Sewing Meeting, Women's Own, Wesley Guild, Brigades - Girls and Boys - and Band. Similarly, half-hour concerts were arranged by the Choir and the Sunday School; and competitions, such as billiards, bowls, loop-ball, candle-lighting, feeding the cat, table tennis, hat trimming (men only) and nail driving (ladies only) were arranged by the Young Men's Institute.

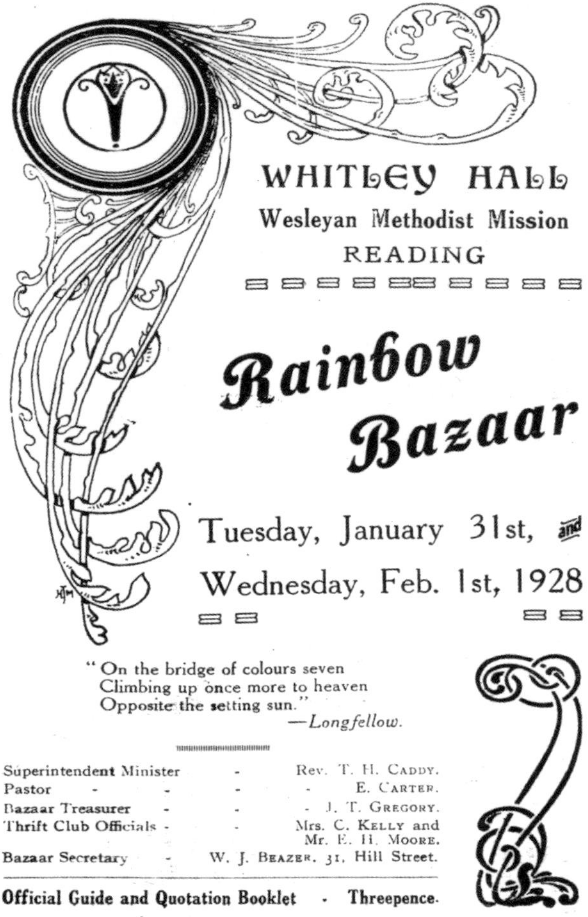

WHITLEY HALL
Wesleyan Methodist Mission
READING

Rainbow Bazaar

Tuesday, January 31st, and
Wednesday, Feb. 1st, 1928

"On the bridge of colours seven
Climbing up once more to heaven
Opposite the setting sun."
—*Longfellow.*

Superintendent Minister	Rev. T. H. Caddy.
Pastor	E. Carter.
Bazaar Treasurer	J. T. Gregory.
Thrift Club Officials	Mrs. C. Kelly and Mr. E. H. Moore.
Bazaar Secretary	W. J. Beazer, 31, Hill Street.

Official Guide and Quotation Booklet - Threepence.

Also, from the table, it can be seen that the Boys' Life Brigade did not maintain its initial popularity as numbers halved to 20 boys and 3 officers in just one year despite the granting of several requests to the Brigade in its first few years after its inauguration. These included the granting of permission on *July 6th, 1909*, for collecting cards for funds toward the purchase of two bugles. On *October 5th* of the same year, they were also given permission to hold Bible and other Classes on Thursdays for one and a half hours in the upstairs classroom and allowed to form a Drum and Fife Band, arrange two Saturday evening concerts and make arrangements for their Anniversary.

Similarly, the Management Committee began to make requests of the Brigade - they were invited to attend meetings from *February 16th, 1909* then, on *April 19th, 1910,* they were asked to provide a display at the Summer Gathering in Cintra Grounds, or failing that at Leighton Park. However, by *January 18th, 1910*, the *Management Committee* agreed that a letter should be sent to the Captain of the Boys' Life Brigade "calling attention to the behaviour of the lads in disturbing meetings and being insolent to the Hallkeeper and asking that they be under an efficient Officer who shall be responsible for their behaviour and that they be admitted by their right entrance. It was agreed to ask the Boys' Life Brigade to start their Band practice at 7.30."

By *November 3rd, 1911*, according to the *Minutes of an informal Leaders' Meeting*, there was much discussion, and then it was unanimously agreed that a Company of the Boys' Brigade be started at the Hall at once as the BLB had practically ceased to exist. Second thoughts were expressed by *November 7th* when it was felt that the starting of a Boys' Brigade had been proceeded with in undue haste. However, by *November 17th*, it was agreed to proceed with the formation of a company of the Boys' Brigade after all.

Unfortunately, we do not have a continuous record of *Minutes of meetings* connected with Whitley Hall so it is not clear what happened next. However, Len Rapley recalled:

"I became a member of the 1st Reading Company Boys' Life Brigade which was attached to Whitley Hall when it was formed (or reformed) in 1913. The officers then were Captain George Dixon and Lieutenants Bob Wells and Frank Hamblin. At the beginning, most of the time was occupied with drilling and learning First Aid, which was taught us by Fred Coppuck, who later became Superintendent of the Reading St John's Ambulance Brigade.

"When the bugles and drums arrived, we had to learn how to play them, then, after many weird noises and perseverance, we managed to master two small marching tunes to which we put the following words:

1. Here comes the Boys' Brigade all smothered in marmalade,
   A tu-penny ha-penny pill box, half a yard of braid.
2. Fall in A, fall in B, fall in all the comp-a-ny.

"Only a few First Aid badges and two stripes - one to myself - had been awarded and things were getting into full swing, when, owing to the Captain's pressure of war work and the 'calling up' of Lieutenant Frank Hamblin to the Forces, there was no option but to disband for the duration of the War. I seem to remember there being a company attached to each of the following Churches - Wesley, Elm Park Hall and, I believe, Caversham.

"When the company was eventually reformed in 1924, I was appointed a Lieutenant with the other officers being Captain Bob Wells, Senior Lieutenant Harold Moore and Lieutenants Stan Morris and Fred Giddings. I was not able to hold that position for long owing to my late hours of working - 'til 7 pm each evening except Friday when it was 8 pm and Saturday 9 pm."

The next available *Minutes of the Leaders' Meeting* are those for *March 9th, 1922 to December 1st, 1933*. These confirm the latter part of Len's description because, for *May 19th, 1924*, we again read of the starting up of a company of the Boys' Life Brigade. At that time, Mr Cloke spoke of the pressing need of such an organisation being formed and it was unanimously agreed that permission be granted for same to be started. Mr Dixon and Mr Giles were elected to represent the Leaders' Meeting on the Brigade Council and the following were elected Officers: Captain A R Wells, Senior Lieutenant H Moore and Lieutenants S Morris, F Giddings and L Rapley.

By *September 22nd* of that year, in answer to a question, Mr Cloke reported that the Boys' Life Brigade had fully justified its formation and, by *January 26th, 1925*, a letter was read from the Sunday School Secretary regarding the starting of a Company of the Girls' Life Brigade. Mr Cloke again made a stirring appeal on the children's behalf and the following were elected as officers: Captain Miss Dorothy Fry and Lieutenants Miss Violet Morris and Miss Agnes Dixon, with representatives to the GLB Council being Mrs Porter and Miss M Cummins.

One of those Lieutenants, whose father, George Dixon, was Boys' Brigade Captain for many years, became A Rosa Wilson. She described a display with a fire-fighting item which took place in the Large Schoolroom: "There was a large canvas tube attached to the gallery, down which we were able to slide. We also enjoyed route marches with the boys. Later I became an officer in the Girls' Brigade with Dorothy Wells and Vi Moore."

From its inception, there was much co-operation between the GLB and the BLB to the extent that they had a joint Anniversary from April, 1926, and were both asked to sing carols at the Christmas morning service in the same year. Displays were kept separate, though, as February 9th and 16th were requested for 1927.

Raymond Searle, whose parents were life-long members of Spring Gardens Mission and Whitley Hall and whose father was a Chapel Steward for many years, passed through the ranks of the Boys' Brigade under Captain Wells and was finally Lieutenant to Captain Reg Sherwood, who was his cousin. A photograph taken in Whitley Hall before the last war showed the then minister in charge, Pastor Dear, with Reg Sherwood on his right and Raymond on his left with Den Petty seated at the right end of the row.

Another initially very popular organisation, which, like the PSA, did not survive at Whitley Hall, is the Wesley Guild. Three months after its formation, it was reported as having 107 members in 1909. However, it seems to have ceased meeting 40 years later after it was stated at the *AGM* on *Thursday, April 21st, 1949* that: "The President then referred to an earlier meeting of the Guild when it was intimated that it would be a great improvement in every way if the Guild could merge with other Youth organisations of Whitley Hall and meet two nights a week instead of one as hitherto thus effecting an economy in staff and making the best possible use of available accommodation."

From the *Minutes* which have survived *since 1930*, we can see that the membership then was 117, an increase of nine members over the previous year.

There had been an average attendance of: 55 for the whole session
46 on Devotional evenings,
51 on Christian Service evenings
53 on Literary
and 91 on Social evenings.

As well as an overall president - Pastor Spargo - there was a secretary and an assistant secretary. For each of the Devotional, Christian Service and Literary sections, there were vice presidents, secretaries and pianists. In addition there was a roll secretary, magazine secretary, badge secretary, Tennis Club financial secretary and a Look Out Secretary and committee. A treasurer, auditor and caterer completed the roles.

I was intrigued by the term 'Look Out Secretary'. However, the term became clear from the entry on *August 24th, 1931* when, in a *Minute of the Executive Meeting*, it was stated: "A group of Lookers Out (three men and three women) were appointed to assist Mr G North in securing new members for the Guild."

Some indication of the type of activities organised by the Guild can be gleaned from the *letter* mentioned in the *Executive Committee meeting* held on *September 7th, 1930.* In it the Guild members were invited to debate with Wesley Men's League on: "Pacifism is the only sure way to World Peace." In that instance, the Guild had to propose and second the opposition.

A play performed that year, *Farley Goes Out*, was obviously so well appreciated by its audiences that the Salvation Army in the Butts asked the cast if they would repeat it for them. Unfortunately, owing to the difficulty of hiring costumes and the expense, the Guild Executive felt compelled to decline the invitation.

According to the programme, which cost 1/- (ie one shilling = 5p in present currency), the performance was held on "Thursday, January 9th. Doors open 7-0. Be seated 7-35 for 7-45" as part of The Circuit Crusade of the Wesleyan Methodist Church. The play was written by F Pratt Green who is perhaps now better known for his hymn writing, 27 of which appeared in *Hymns & Psalms* when it was published in 1983. It is summarised as "A Conflict of Ideals. The Younger generation against the Older. The West against the East. Christ Conquers all."

Dr Leslie F Church, BA described the play as "no mere pageant. The argument is presented with a fine dramatic sense, and the appeal to mind and heart is well sustained and strongly reasoned. In the first act the scene is laid in an English market town in 1750, and is concerned with the rescue of John Wesley from a mob. His deliverer is found in an unexpected quarter. The other two acts deal with the modern outlook. Inherited Methodist traditions - the influence of a good woman and the vocation of her son - are the main factors. The complex reaction is further directed by the finely conceived character of a Hindu student . . . There are few missionary plays of so distinguished a character."

Cast of *Farley Goes Out* in Whitley Hall Church with Pastor Spargo and W Maynard 5th & 6th from left in back row. Main characters are in the front row, being (from left): Percy Hunter, William Gregory, Ivy Tuffield, Tom Joy, George Dixon, Agnes Dixon, Rosa Dixon, George Cloke, Doris White, Ernest Wilson, John Hunter, Ronald Bailey.

In 1931, the question of rambles was raised and it was agreed that four should be held during the summer - two on Wednesdays and two on Saturdays. It was also agreed that the Guild should support the Church Open Air Meetings, nominally once a month. The rambles during that summer were to "Bear

Wood on Wednesday, June 24th; to Streatley on Saturday, July 18th; to Mapledurham on Wednesday, August 19th; and Peppard on Saturday, September 12th; also to Henley on August Bank Holiday."

Obviously the rambles proved popular because an extra one to the Hardwicke Estate was held on Saturday, October 3rd and the Ramble Committee immediately planned four for Saturdays and two for Wednesdays for the following year. The rambles remained popular and in *1937* the following comment was made: "Summer rambles had proved such happy events that the meeting decided to support Three Mile Cross Harvest, this constituting a further ramble."

By *September 5th, 1935*, the Tennis Club had a full membership of 25 and the outstanding features of its season were reported as being:

1. The change of ground to Northumberland Avenue, following an offer by Mr Cox and
2. The reduction of the lost ball menace.

On September 10th, 1997, when she was approaching her 90th birthday but still a very active member of Whitley Hall, Gladys Clifford recalled that the Tennis Club had first met behind Gregory's Shop in Shinfield Road. After moving to the rear of Cox's Silver Coaches in Northumberland Avenue, it finally moved to behind 8, Christchurch Gardens and then ceased during the Second World War when the men were called up for the forces.

At an *Executive Meeting* on *September 11th, 1933*, evenings for "Home Missions, Foreign Missions (Play), League of Nations, the Survey of the Gambling Problem, Temperance and visits from Pastor Spargo's Class and Mr. Cloke's Class" were arranged. Socials in 1937 had the themes "At Home, Old Favourites, Gipsy and Song Titles".

It is interesting to note that size in itself was not considered the most important issue by Chapel Stewards when the Guild requested that they be allowed to change rooms with the Boys' Brigade "as the latter only declared a membership of 17 at their Council." The Stewards offered the use of part of the Large Hall (ie the Church) "suitably warmed, lighted and curtained off" for evenings when the Small Schoolroom would be inadequate.

Chapter XI: Bridge over Troubled Waters

Time, like an ever-rolling stream
Bears all its sons away.
They fly forgotten as a dream
Dies at the opening day.

Verse 6 of no 358 in Hymns & Psalms
by Isaac Watts (1674 - 1748)

There are no references to the first wars that took place during the development of the Spring Gardens area of Reading in the 19th century. According to J M Guilding, who was Vicar of St Laurence when he compiled his *Notable Events in Reading* in 1895, there was the War with China in 1841 and the War with Russia in 1854. The latter was more commonly known as the Crimean War and possibly most remembered for Florence Nightingale's contribution to nursing its wounded. Since then, there has been the South African War from 1899 - 1902, which is more usually known as the Boer War because it involved the Dutch farmers. However, the First World War of 1914 - 1918 is within living memory of our nonagenarians. Len Rapley, whose reminiscences of the Spring Gardens area and of Whitley Hall's Boys' Life Brigade are described in the previous two chapters, had this to say, in 1986, about the First World War and how it affected his life:

"I was 12 years old when the war broke out and attended Whitley Hall Sunday School throughout. There we gave considerable time and effort to raising funds for Foreign Missions and the National Children's Homes and rehearsing for anniversaries etc.

"I joined the Boys' Brigade when it was formed shortly before the outbreak of war, but, soon after, it had to be disbanded when one Officer was called up and the others were involved in the war effort. At the time that happened, the Brigade was just getting into full swing. Two stripes had been awarded - one of which was to myself - and the Bugle Band had just mastered two tunes, the words put to one being:

'Here comes the Boys' Brigade, all smothered in marmalade,
A tuppenny ha'penny pillbox, half a yard of braid.'

"During the Sunday evening services in the 'Chapel', those who were away were always remembered, and the hymn:

'Holy Father, in Thy mercy,
Hear our anxious prayer.
Keep our loved ones, now far distant,
'Neath Thy care'

was invariably sung. Uniforms of all Services could be seen in the congregation, proudly worn by those home on leave. From time to time we would hear of someone being called up and occasionally of others who would not return. Wounded soldiers who were convalescent at 'Sutherlands' in Christchurch Road were often entertained in the Small Schoolroom at parties arranged by the Women's Own and were regularly invited into our homes.

"Mention must be made of Pastor Alan Stocking who was such an inspiration and comfort to many during those days. He was greatly loved and respected. Several important events in my life took place during those war years - I left school and commenced work, was recruited into the Territorial Army whilst still only 13 years of age, and met my future wife, Anne.

To Pastor Bert Bailey

August 23rd 1922.

The members and friends of the Wesleyan Mission at Whitley Hall, Reading, desire to express their sincere appreciation of the earnest and efficient work you have done during the two years you have been in charge of this Mission.

They recognise the difficulties, which indifferent health and the present social conditions have imposed upon you and regret circumstances prevent the continuation of your work among them.

They value very highly the kindly interest in all sections of the work which you and Mrs Bailey have always shown and ask your joint acceptance of the accompanying gift.

Their prayers and interest will follow you both in your changed sphere of life, and they pray that GODS richest blessing may continue to rest upon you.

Signed on behalf of Church and Congregation.

Geo. H. Dixon.
J. H. Gregory.

"Pastor Bert Bailey, who followed Pastor Stocking, was particularly interested in us young ones. He was said to have been a boxer in his earlier days. In addition to the reforming of the Boys' Life Brigade, as it was known in those days, and in which I was an officer for a time, he was instrumental in forming a Youth Club, which also met on Friday evenings and I had the honour of being its first secretary. There was no 'unruly element' then!"

There is an impressive Roll of Honour of those who served in the 1914 - 1918 War. It hung on the back wall of Whitley Hall Methodist Church until the building was sold in November, 1997 but it now hangs in Christ Church in Christchurch Road, Reading. Since the members of both congregations have met together around the War Memorial in the grounds of that church each Armistice Day, then each Remembrance Day, since 1920, it seemed most appropriate that it should find a new home there.

Among the 17 names on the Roll of Honour is that of my own paternal grandfather, Albert Barnes who served in the Royal Horse Artillery. He was one of the fortunate ones who was neither wounded nor killed in action. Of the 33 shown as wounded, 16 either died later of their wounds or were killed in action, namely:

W Adnams	Reginald Brill	Walter Brill	Ed L Cocks
Thos H Cooper	Harold Cooper	A W Eames	Reginald Edington
Ernest Filewood	Chas Heath	Thos Heath	Wilfred Allen
Thos Porter	A G Taylor	W Townsend	Jos W Wells

The War Memorial at Christ Church was referred to by its vicar, the Rev J F Warren, during the account of the *14th Anniversary services of Whitley Hall in 1920.* At that time, he is reported as mentioning that that particular Wednesday evening meeting was not the first time that Christ Church and Whitley Hall had shaken hands together. "When, rather more than a year ago, his own people had asked him to call a meeting to decide what memorial they should put up to the fallen in the war his first thought had been: 'Shall we ask our friends at Whitley Hall if they would like to join in?' He hoped that the cross in the Churchyard would be ready in two months' time and that, on the occasion of its unveiling, his friend Pastor Stocking, would stand beside him in the Churchyard and that as many of his audience as possible would attend the services."

As he put it: "Thus they had joined hands over their immortal dead; how much more fitting that they should amalgamate forces in a conflict and a warfare that was immeasurably more important than even the great war that had just passed. That war was but an episode, a passing hour, in the greater war that stretched back through the ages . . . He would not insult them by saying that there were no differences between them, but they must leave those differences in the hands of their joint God. Their cause was the same, the cause of truth and righteousness. They had, first and foremost, one Lord and Master. That was the meaning of Whitley Hall and that was the meaning of Christ Church. You in your way and we in ours are trying, with how many imperfections and with what faltering steps! to solve the same problems."

To this day, the congregations of both Whitley Methodist and Christ Church meet around that same memorial on Remembrance Sunday, despite the fact that a period of two minutes' silence is no longer observed by passing traffic. Similarly, remembering the eleventh hour of the eleventh day of the eleventh month when the Armistice was signed after the First World War was replaced by a National Day of Remembrance for those who died in both World Wars. Since 1956, the latter has been fixed as the second Sunday in November.

There is very little reference to either of the wars in the minutes of the church activities throughout their entirety. However, a special *Committee of the Women's Own* was called on *September 12th, 1939* "owing to the outbreak of war to decide Anniversary arrangements. It was decided to cancel the evening meeting owing to blackout and the W.O. Choir to sing Sunday morning and afternoon and Mrs McKinley be asked to sing Wed. aft. instead of Wed. night - other arrangements to stand."

The next reference to the Second World War was given in the *June 7th, 1940 Minutes of Committee* in which: "The Secretary told the Committee that she would not be standing for re-election owing to distance and war conditions etc." By *September 3rd, 1940*: "Rev Priestly in a few words thanked all who had helped by their attendance to keep the meetings going under war conditions." It seems this included the annual outing and New Year Social.

However, some things did have to be changed. The Secretary called the Committee together on *April 29th, 1941* "to ask whether a grant could be made available from W.O. Funds towards the Forces Comforts Funds now being started at the Hall. All readily agreed that we should do our part." Also, on *June 9th, 1942*, when the secretary reported that she had been approached by Mr H Moore as to whether the W.O. could manage a stall for the Church Garden Party as in previous years. "All agreed it was almost impossible this year owing to rationing etc but agreed to attend the Garden Party and give it full support."

The first indirect reference to the Second World War in the *Minutes of the Whitley Hall Wesleyan Mission Choir* appeared on *June 6th, 1940* under Concert Committee, where it was reported:
"Refreshments consisting of tea and coffee (audience to bring own sugar) sausage rolls and cakes. No sandwiches owing to butter ration."
Then again on *July 11th* of the same year:
"Owing to rationing difficulties, it was proposed by Mr Morris that we cancel the Social suggested for November 1st. Seconded by Mr Purnell."

However, although not mentioned in Whitley Hall Minutes, it is apparent from the *Centenary Souvenir Brochure of Wesley Methodist Church, Reading (1973)* that the 1939 - 1945 War did bring about changes in the ministerial arrangements within the Circuit probably rather quicker than might otherwise have been envisaged. According to Rev Leonard Babb, who had become superintendent of the Wesleyan Circuit two years before the outbreak of war, he had foreseen the possibilities that could result from the union of London Street and Wesley at that time. This was helped when, in 1938, the ministers of both the London Street Primitive Methodist Circuit and the Wesley Wesleyan Circuit had found that they could work well together when rehearsing for a Ministers' Concert suggested by Elm Park Hall's newly-arrived Pastor, J B Button.

When war broke out, one of the London Street ministers - a Territorial Army Chaplain - was called up and there was no hope of a replacement. Since Wesley Church could not be blacked out but London Street Church could, it was obvious that the congregations should unite - with the morning service at Wesley and the evening one at London Street. This arrangement worked so well that at the *Wesley Leaders' Meeting* held on *15th December, 1939*, Rev Babb suggested that London Street should be invited to join them in forming a New Society called Queen's Road. By the end of September, 1940, the concluding services had been held at London Street in thanksgiving for the 74 years' Christian Witness in that Church.

Prior to September 1940, Whitley Hall was in the Wesley Circuit along with ten other Churches viz Wesley, Oxford Road, Elm Park Hall, Caversham, Tilehurst, Caversham Heights, Wokingham, Henley, Three Mile Cross and Kentwood. However, after the amalgamation of the Wesley and London Street Circuits in 1940, the churches were grouped under the pastoral care of a member of the ministerial staff as follows:

1. Wesley	London Street	
2. Oxford Road	Friar Street	Woodcote
3. Two Cavershams	Henley	Gallows Tree Common
4. Whitley Hall	Swallowfield	Three Mile Cross
5. West Reading	Elm Park Hall	Burghfield
6. Cumberland Road	Wokingham	
7. Tilehurst	Pangbourne	Kentwood.

Returning to references about the war in *Whitley Hall's Minutes*, we discover that it was not until *May 29th, 1941* that there are references to men being called up and to other difficulties caused by the War:
"The arrangements for the Concert being left to the Concert Committee. Miss E Dyer was elected to this Committee where Mrs Studley had previously served and Mrs R Winch in place of her husband, now serving with H.M. Forces.
Social - Owing to difficulties in catering etc, it was thought wise to leave the Social over until more favourable times.
Outing - Owing to Charabanc Companies not taking bookings for pleasure trips this year it was proposed by Mrs Prince and seconded by Miss G Prince that enquiries be made as to the possibility of a Steamer Trip for Wednesday July 16th."
[Editorial note: I was particularly interested to read this as Gwen Prince and her mother lived next door to my family when we lived at 232, Basingstoke Road]

Similarly, it was not until *August 21st, 1941* that there was any mention of the blackout: "Meeting of Choir Members for practice during blackout. Mr Morris proposed and Mrs Dyer seconded that we meet for practice on the moonlight nights which would be about two practices per month, the Choirmaster to announce on the Sunday a practice for the following Thursday."

Then, at the General Meeting on *April 16th, 1942*: "It was proposed by Mr Morris and seconded by Mrs Thompson that as the evenings were now light we start our weekly Thursday night practice and try to turn up in good numbers."

It was towards the end of the war before it was mentioned as such in the *Choir Minutes*, namely at the General Meeting held on *May 10th, 1944*:
"Proposed and seconded that choir outing and Social be left until after the War."

Indirect references to the war were not confined to the choir. In the *Minutes of The Whitley Hall Wesley Guild* on *April 15th, 1940*, it was stated:
"Rev J C Priestly presided and 23 other members were present. The Secretary in his report bore record of the faithfulness of the Officers in difficult times and of the valued services of Speakers week by week." Although a rummage sale was held that year on May 18th, a year later on *April 21st, 1941*, the comment was made that: "The matter of a Rummage Sale was considered impracticable in the prevailing circumstances and was left for the current session."

Even after the war, restrictions continued to apply, and, on July 10th, 1947, it was recorded: "The Committee agreed that owing to the serious food situation a supper would be out of the question."

The Roll of Honour for the 1939 - 1945 War, which is also now in Christ Church, showed that there were 55 men of the Church on active service and ten men and women in the Auxiliary Services. Of those, just two were killed or died on active service - Stanley Kybird and Raymond Seymour - quite a contrast to the 16 who were killed during the First World War.

One of those mentioned in the Roll of Honour for the Second World War, Robert Cooper, wrote the following memories for *Newslink* just after he and his wife, Eva, moved to Eye, Suffolk in 1987. Throughout *1988*, Bob's recollections of his experiences at Whitley Hall were serialised and for the *September /October* edition, he wrote:

"I joined the RAF in October 1941 and, when I said farewell to Rev Priestly, he handed me a Methodist Passport to introduce me to any Church that I visited. I used this on numerous occasions at many different Churches throughout England, Scotland and in Wales, and in the two places in Wales where the services were conducted wholly in the native tongue, the Minister spoke in English so that I could understand.

"Eva and I fixed our wedding date for the 24th June, 1944. For some reason the British and American High Command omitted to inform me that the Invasion of Europe would have started by then and, of course, my Application for Leave was promptly tossed out. After much pleading and crawling on my knees to various superior Officers, one of them took pity on me and generously granted me a thirty-six hour Pass and, with a little rule bending, I managed to stretch it to forty-eight hours. The fact that the nearest railway station was 14 miles away didn't help. Still at least we were married, ably so by the Rev Priestly in his own inimitable manner.

"The War dragged on and, when it was over, nobody was in any hurry to get rid of us and so it was, in September 1946, that I was handed an ill-fitting suit and an equally ill-fitting hat (which was never worn, incidentally!) and, with no regrets, waved the RAF 'Goodbye'. Like many thousands more, I returned to Civvy Street full of the joys of spring, thinking that everything would be the same as when we left. How wrong could we be! Everything had changed!

"By this time, the Rev Wilf White was resident Minister at Whitley Hall and I must say that he did all in his power to make our return welcome. Some will doubtless remember his 'Living Statuary', which took up the whole of the floor space in the Church and was attended by hundreds and was a great success."

The Living Statuary mentioned by Bob took place in 1948 and is my own first recollection of an event connected with Whitley Hall. As a four-year old, I was the youngest person involved and was a Cherub with the then minister's daughter, Margaret White. We were part of the Nativity tableau which was positioned in the altar area and the only thing that I can remember about it was that I was given icecream as a reward for staying still for so long!

Photographs of the event show that the whole of the Church was decorated with tableaux of Biblical scenes and I have since been given two complete sets of the photographs in albums, obviously much treasured over the years. A *Guide to the Living Statuary* states "This is a sacred exhibition and your co-operation in helping to maintain the right atmosphere will be greatly appreciated. You are particularly requested NOT TO STAND STILL but to move slowly and quietly through the Church". The tableaux were then listed as:

WEST END

The Nativity - see photograph above (it includes the author!)

SOUTH SIDE

The finding of Moses — Rebecca at the Well
The Lost Coin — The Lost Sheep
The Prodigal's Return
"And they brought young children to Him"

EAST END

The Vigil — The Angelus
The Christian Virtues - Faith, Hope, Love & Joy

NORTH SIDE

The Gate Beautiful	Hannah, Samuel and Eli
Loaves and Fishes	Ruth and Naomi
The Widow's Mite	Abraham and Isaac

CENTRE

"All nations shall come and worship before Him"

I was also recently able to date the event exactly because I came across a book entitled 'Baby Moses' which had inscribed in it:

"With a big THANK YOU to Daphne Barnes for being such a good girl in the Living Statuary at Whitley Hall on November 3rd & 4th, 1948."

However, it was Pauline Crump's move to King's Lynn in 1999 (she was previously mentioned in connection with Whitley Hall's choir in chapter VII) that enabled me to discover more about the event. Going to a service at London Road Methodist Church in that town the first Sunday after her move, she was introduced to Liz White when she mentioned that she was from Reading. Liz turned out to be the elder daughter of Rev Wilf White and, in a letter dated 25th February, 2000, she had this to say about the Living Statuary, in which she took part as one of the children in the 'And They brought young children to Him' tableau:

"My father trailed round borrowing things – the barrow, pampas grass etc. The lamb came from a butcher's shop in Christchurch Green and most things were painted white to give the impression of stone carvings – hence statuary - and the people were dressed in white – living statuary. Nobody moved (except the cherubs!). This stillness had to be maintained for a long while as crowds walked round looking at us. Modern people, particularly children, would not do it. Think of Tony Wells and Derek Allen maintaining their poses in 'The Prodigal's Return' and 'The Gate Beautiful'. Also, if you look at the photos, you can see the intensity of gaze, particularly between people who had to look at each other. There was a terrific atmosphere."

Other special events that Liz recalled from her Whitley Hall days were:
"My father arranged a recital by the African organist, Fella Suwandi, who was the organist at Kingsway Central Hall with Donald Soper. I remember Fella

well as he was a very colourful and vibrant personality.

"On several occasions, a member of the Forces, possibly an airman, used to perform at the church with his band or group. I'm pretty sure that it was Henry Mancini.

"My father had a friend who was a missionary in Sierra Leone, Rev Kenneth Nicholson. He came to stay with us and preached at Whitley Hall. He used to bring wonderful craft work from Sierra Leone to bring alive the continent to his listeners.

"The Vicar at Christ Church, somewhere very near The Mount, where Whitley Hall's Manse was in those days, was Just-de-Blanc who became Bishop of Stepney. He had a housekeeper called Margaret from Holland so we called her Dutch Margaret. I'm sure that she attended Whitley Hall and she was very interesting. They had had a terrible time in Holland; their home was taken over by the Germans and the family lived in the back room and had to cook for the Germans who had the best food."

Other recollections about life when her father was Minister at Whitley Hall included the Candlelit Carol Service that he started at Christmas as he had at every church in which he served and which all have retained to this day. She also commented:

"I do remember Sunday School, ascending dark stairs in the Hall behind the church, walking along a narrow and gloomy corridor. At the end of the corridor there was a small room to the left and a larger room ahead. In the larger room stood Mrs Jane Joy, awaiting us with a serene smile, regardless of how badly we behaved! The patience of a qualified Infant Teacher! I remember rehearsing a play or presentation from a book. I think it was *If Jesus came to my house* (a Joan Gale Thomas book). It ran 'If Jesus came to my house and knocked upon the door, I'm sure I'd be more happy than I've ever been before.' It went all through the day and led onto what we do for others in His name.

"As we walked to church we gathered up people between the Mount and Whitley Hall, lastly the Joy Family, who, if I recall, lived in a corner house quite near the church. At that time they used to still sound the air raid sirens. I remember being terrified and I thought it came from the roof of a large house we used to pass. The roof was a dome, turquoise green. It was probably on a tower or turret but I could only think this wail came from there and I dreaded walking past it. It was near the church as I recall.

"Also during that time the Olympics were held in England and the runner with the Olympic torch ran through Reading. I saw this – was it near the church? I don't recall if I walked to the location but I have very little memory of car riding; my father needed his allocation of petrol (coupons) for church business." [Editorial comment: I know the Olympic torch runner ran past what was then The Four Horseshoes public house as we lived opposite at 232 Basingstoke Road and my father stressed the importance of the event to my two year old brother and myself. I should therefore assume that the runner continued up the Basingstoke Road, past Whitley Hall and towards Reading town centre.]

As well as those recollections, Liz sent a photograph of her father which had appeared in the Methodist Recorder in their 'Recorder's Pictures of the Century' feature at the end of 1999. The photo was taken at the 1948 Methodist Conference, which was held in Bristol and to which her father travelled from Whitley Hall. He is pictured shaking hands with the first elected woman Vice President of Conference.

Chapter XII: Flushed with Success

O teach me, Lord, that I may teach
The precious things Thou dost impart;
And wing my words that they may reach
The hidden depths of many a heart.

Verse 4 of no 553 in Hymns & Psalms
by Frances Ridley Havergal (1836 - 79)

The oldest recollections of Sunday School relate only to Whitley Hall and were recalled by octagenarian Len Rapley in 1986 for the 80th anniversary of the Sunday School in those buildings. He wrote:

"I was nearly four years old at the time of the opening of Whitley Hall. My mother was at the ceremony and later told me that mine was one of the first names placed on the Cradle Roll.

"As soon as I was old enough, I was taken to the Primary Department of the Sunday School where Miss Gladys Hine was in charge. She played the piano and taught us little plays and country dancing. One play I particularly remember was 'Ride with Mr Dream-man'. It included 'Put on your nighties and say your prayers', but some of us boys preferred the term 'nightshirts'!

"The small text cards given to us each Sunday by our teacher were greatly prized. Some of our favourite hymns in those early years were:

I think when I read that sweet story of old
Jesus bids us shine
Jesus wants me for a sunbeam
There's a home for little children
God who hath made the daisies
Jesus loves me, this I know.

"The big occasion was undoubtedly the Sunday School treat held at Leighton Park each year on a Wednesday afternoon in August during the school holidays. Us infants were transported in horse-drawn carts owned by Mr

Honey and Bert Peck (greengrocers) and Mr Pounds (furniture remover). When there, we took part in a few games and races and very much enjoyed our tea. I have never forgotten the large slice of slab fruit cake which we were given. It was later known to us as 'School cake'.

"These were particularly happy days.

"Later in the Senior School with Mr George Cloke, Superintendent, we put on many plays in aid of Missionary and other funds. One I particularly remember is 'The Nigger Parliament' and I can still repeat my speech (which he did for the author of this book on October 2nd, 1990, soon after his eighty-eighth birthday). Weekly collections were also made for Missionary funds - boys and girls being counted separately. There were two ladders hung on the wall over the platform, being climbed by a boy and a girl, indicating the amount collected. The girl was always on a higher rung as can be seen in the following photo.

From left, back row: Hilda Griffin, Florrie Morris, Irene Coppuck, Rose Morris. Middle row: Cissie Coppuck, Len Rapley, Ellen Swindon, Stan Morris, Jane Dixon, Morley Waite, Agnes Dixon. Front row: Doris & Fred Cox, Margaret Cloke.

"Efforts were also made on behalf of the National Children's Homes. I remember these being very much increased when Winnie Dyer was admitted after the death of her father. I also remember that there was a Roll of Honour which hung on the platform wall and was illuminated by gas lighting. Included on it was the name of Edward Dyer, father of Winnie and Edna. On the same wall was a framed prayer, which read:

Morning Prayer

Our Father in Heaven, who in Thy loving kindness hast given us all the good things that come to us, help us to be truthful as we bring our words of thanks to Thee, and when we sing our songs of praise, help us by Thy Good Spirit to be sincere: may we mean all we say. Help us this day to be kind, to be thoughtful, to be noble.

For Jesus' sake,
AMEN

"A very important day each year was the Sunday School Anniversary when special Services were held in the Chapel, as it was known in those days. This was particularly so in the morning when we usually had a special Preacher, hymns, music and plays. The choir seats and platform were filled to capacity with us children. It was usual for the older children to attend the Morning Service after Sunday School so we were often at Whitley Hall for two hours (or more!) in the morning and then were back for more Sunday School in the afternoon.

"Still the School treat at Leighton Park was the big occasion. We would march there, headed by a few of the Spring Gardens Band, which was attached to Whitley Hall. As we passed the Queen's Head Public House in Christchurch Road, we would shout: 'Shut up the Public Houses, we're all Teetotallers here!' and sing those same words to the tune of 'For he's a jolly good fellow'. Many of us had 'signed the Pledge' and were members of the Little White Ribboners.

"When once we arrived at Leighton Park, we took part in a number of races, including:

Egg and spoon	Three-legged	Obstacle	Thread needle

We also had a good tea in relays. The Band played music during the evening, when those who had been working during the afternoon joined us, and there was bowling for a live pig. As it was getting dusk we would wend our weary way home.

"Much preparation went into the Scripture Examination which was taken each year. It seemed that the Country Shield was nearly always won by Shinfield Free Church and the Town one by Elm Park Hall. Teachers I particularly remember from my Sunday School days are Bob Wells, Jim Morris and Albert Coppuck, who became known as 'Albie can't swim'. I also think of one Sunday afternoon when we were waiting in the Vestry for Mr Morris to take a class and one boy placed a Bible on top of the door so that it would fall on him as he entered. However, just as he was about to come in, another boy replaced it with a Bible Box. Amazingly, it remained balanced! Later, Mr Morris became Choir Master, Mr Wells Captain of the Boys' Brigade and Mr Coppuck Caretaker.

"I mustn't forget my close friends of those days, viz Stan Morris, Morley Waite, Bill Gregory and George Winch, and those who were Ministers during my time at Whitley Hall - Pastor Alan Stocking, who was much loved by all, and Pastors Bert Bailey and Fred Thorpe. Two favourite hymns of later days were:

Jesus shall reign where'er the sun & Summer suns are glowing

"During our later years at Sunday School, Mr Cloke would take some of us on country rambles. On Good Fridays, we would go to either Burghfield Common or Mortimer Common then have tea in the Mitford Hall at Three Mile Cross and attend a Service in the Chapel there in the evening. Mr Cloke was an excellent photographer and the majority of the photographs that survive today were taken by him.

"I went on to become a member of the Chapel Choir, an Officer in the Boys' Brigade, Secretary of the Young Men's Institute when it was founded by Pastor Bert Bailey, and a member of the Spring Gardens Prize Band. In 1928, I moved to Park Congregational Church where I joined the Choir and Choral Society and married Anne Coppuck whom I had met in the Whitley Hall Sunday School."

One of Len's fellow members of the Sunday School, Agnes Dixon, who moved to Sutton and preferred to use her second Christian name with her married surname and be known as A Rosa Wilson, was surprised to find that her 80th year was also the 80th of Whitley Hall Sunday School. She commented in reply to an article by the cartoonist, 'AREFF' (Ron R Fennell) in the *April 25th, 1985* edition of the *Reading Standard*, in which he drew his impression of an outing of a Whitley Hall Sunday School treat of 1918:

"I fear Areff is wrong as we never would have had a treat on a Sunday. He mentions treats in Leighton Park, but I can go further back than that. We used to march with the Spring Gardens Prize Band along Whiteknights Road to Foxhill, the home of Sir Rufus Isaacs.

"Marching home, the older children carried Chinese lanterns on long poles. The lanterns were about ten inches high, made of paper and they squashed down flat. They had a night light or candle inside and were carried on a long bamboo rod. I longed for the day when I could carry one, but when I got out of Primary, the 1914 War had begun and the lanterns were banned as an air raid precaution. However, I did hold one of the ropes on our lovely Sunday School banner one year.

"The banner was large - I would say 8 feet wide by over 6 feet high. It had a beautiful rich blue background with a large oval in the centre, with, I think, the Good Shepherd holding a child in his arms. There was a scroll above the oval panel saying 'Whitley Hall Wesleyan Sunday School' and one below it saying 'Suffer the children to come unto me'.

"When we had Sunday School concerts in the Chapel, the 'stage' was made with the trestle tables, and was not too good for country dancing."

Sunday School Concert 1921

Rosa's husband, Ernest, became General Superintendent of the Sunday School when George Cloke died in 1938. At that time, Rosa's sister, Jane Joy, was leader of the Primary Department and Stan Morris and Harold Moore the leaders of the Intermediate and Junior Departments respectively.

Also prior to the 80th Anniversary, 82 year old A E Keep recalled a day outing starting from Whitley Hall in a brake - a large cart drawn by four horses:

"We went to Sir Rufus Isaac's house in Whiteknight's Park by the lake and had tea, buns and games. I believe Sir Rufus was Liberal MP for Reading.

"I went to the Sunday Morning School at Whitley Hall, which we entered from Boult's Walk. My mother sent me every Sunday and we were given a card which the teacher stamped with a red star, so my mother could see that I had been. We lived in Alpha Street then, which ran from Waldeck Street into Mount Street, so it was not far to go, but I had to move 18 years ago when it was pulled down.

"I remember there was a fire at the north side of the Hall. The painter had been burning the paint from the woodwork when it caught light. Now there was a master painter, named Mr Morris, and his family who lived in Southampton Street and used to go to every Service. Also there was a Master plumber and two brothers who lived in Southampton Street as well. They also attended every service and I believe were caretakers at The Hall for a long time, their name being Coppuck."

Reginald Morgan, who lived in Edgehill Street opposite Mr Cloke during his boyhood, was at the same school as 'AREFF' and knew him quite well. He remembered the ride and picking wild flowers in the field and being presented with a toy car, which was made of lead in those days.

Raymond Searle, just a few years younger than Len, observed that he, too, passed through Whitley Hall Sunday School and Boys Brigade:

"I have many memories of Sunday School - appearing in many annual plays performed and I remember that, on Sunday School Anniversary days, my parents always decked me out with a lily of the valley in my buttonhole and I nearly always managed the 104 Stars for maximum attendance. When the annual Summer Treat came round, we all assembled outside Whitley Hall and marched to the grounds of Leighton Park School, where our parents joined us in the evening when the Band played and there were various sideshows. The highlight of the treat was a 'scramble' for sweets thrown from a box by the then Superintendent, Mr Cloke."

During the 14th Anniversary celebrations of Whitley Hall in 1920, it was mentioned that there was special singing by the Sunday School Choir for the Wednesday evening service. Mr Freeman presented a Secretary's report "which abounded with the successes of the past year. Perhaps the most satisfactory feature was the passage dealing with the Sunday School, which is now full to overflowing with 420 scholars."

The Treasurer's balance sheet showed that the year finished with a balance in hand of £73 9*s* 8*d*, as against £10 6*s* 1*d* the previous year. However, he warned them against feeling too optimistic, because, in future, the grants from the Education Committee would be discontinued and the previous year they had amounted to no less than £110.

By 1927, it was mentioned in the *Souvenir of the 21st Anniversary* that "The Sunday School has always been a strong feature. The present Superintendent, G J Cloke, has filled that office with great distinction for 10 years and it continues to prosper. R S Morris, LP, is Secretary (LP denotes that he was a Methodist Local Preacher). Under the recently adopted Graded System, A R Wells and E H Moore are Superintendents of their separate sections. As also Miss Violet Moore in the Primary. We have a great record for our Juvenile Missionary Collecting, and Miss Cummins has done nobly as Secretary; also Morley Waite, assistant. He has now entered the Ministry; W Gregory has succeeded him."

Just before Len Rapley moved to Park Congregational Church, Bob Cooper was introduced to Whitley Hall via its Sunday School and the following were his impressions of those days:

"It was around 1926 when I was first introduced to the Whitley Hall Sunday School, a move largely influenced by my paternal grandfather, a strict Methodist, who had previously attended, with my grandmother, the old Spring Gardens Mission for a number of years.

"The Sunday School in those days was one of the largest in Reading and easily filled the two upstairs rooms, the Small Schoolroom, the Large Schoolroom and the Church. One recalls some of the Leaders who were devoted to the task of moulding and influencing our lives - George Cloke (whose reference was instrumental in securing my first job), Tom and Jane Joy, Ernest Wilson, Harold and Violet Moore, Stan Morris and many more.

The highlights of those days were the treats in Leighton Park - marching there with the Spring Gardens Band in the lead blaring out: 'We all go the same way home'. When, as more senior members, we were given the job of attending the old water boiler for the tea, we could manage, with a little devious stoking, to have flames roaring from the top of the chimney.

"Then there was the Sunday School Anniversary, when, for weeks previously, we had been practising the hymns from the sheet that was to be used on the Great Day. I also recall how, during those practices with Miss Grace Hotson playing the organ, George Stevenson and I were delegated (or volunteered) to pump the organ in the absence of Mr Wilf Flower who normally carried out that duty. How the organ bellows ever withstood our enthusiasm I shall never know! Then on the day of the Anniversary itself there was the parade led by the Spring Gardens Band and Pastor Spargo followed by the entire Sunday School. The route took in the whole of the area near the Church, including Essex Street, Spring Gardens, Collis Street, Waterloo Road and so on.

"It was also at that time of the year that the presentation of books was made for regular attendance. My copy of 'Treasure Island' still stands in the bookcase - a reward for 95 attendances in 1935.

"The Harvest Festival was also a memorable occasion. Those times were not as affluent as they are today and the Harvest gifts, although gladly given, were somewhat menial, consisting mostly of marrows, cabbages, flowers, apples and, from the more well-to-do, perhaps half a dozen eggs. Some will recall that all the produce in those days was auctioned from the pulpit after the week-night Harvest meeting.

"By 1936, when we were older, but by no means wiser, we graduated from Morning School into the Class of Mr Jesse Blunden who exerted a very great influence on our lives. In 1937 it was time to leave the Sunday School as pupils so we became Sunday School teachers. I can only hope that the impact I made on my pupils bore some resemblance to that made on me by my teachers. However, I doubt that as, unlike their's, I am the first to admit that my patience is not of the everlasting type."

Bob's reference to George Cloke and the size of the Sunday School was reiterated in an article in the *Methodist Times*:

"Mr George J Cloke of the Whitley Hall Mission in the Reading (Wesley) Circuit can be described as an enthusiastic worker with the gifts of ability and thoroughness. .He is general superintendent of the Sunday School - the largest in the town, with a staff of seventy teachers and five hundred scholars . . . A fine reflection upon the quality of service is seen in the fact that sixty of the teachers were formerly scholars in the same school, and happy must be the worker and leader who is faithfully supported by many whom he has nurtured in the change from scholar to teacher. Mr Cloke is a successful leader of a society class, the members being teachers in the school he so ably supervises."

George Cloke's popularity can be most readily assessed from the impressive article which appeared in a local newspaper when he died on his 64th birthday from multiple injuries received the previous day when he was knocked down by a Post Office light engineering van in Forbury Road, Reading. Joyce Woodcraft had preserved the article entitled:

"Church Worker's Death
Coroner's Inquiry into Road Accident
The Late Mr G. J. Cloke"

along with a photograph which she had stuck in to the autograph book which she had started on March 21st, 1936, when she was then Joyce Peck and living at 43 Essex Street as she was when she showed me the article on August 12th, 1990. Under the photograph, she had written:

"Mr G.J. Cloke
September, 1938
In remembrance of my Sunday School superintendent
who died suddenly after an accident.
He was a well-known figure
at Whitley Hall and a friend to everyone."

Such an epitaph was indeed evident to me (who had obviously never known him) from the list of 288 people who had been present at his funeral, in addition to 16 family mourners. These had included those who had worked with him at Messrs Sutton & Sons Ltd, where he had been a departmental foreman. As well as members of Whitley Hall, there were representatives from other churches including Tilehurst, London Street, Anderson Sunday School, Elm Park Hall and Oxford Road Methodist Sunday School; three Ministers of Religion apart from the two conducting the funeral service; a doctor and a captain. There were also representatives from the National Commercial Temperance League, Circuit Stewards, Reading Free Church Council, National Children's Home, Reading Temperance Band, London Street Circuit Trustees and the Sunday School Union at the service and 41 wreaths were laid, as well as those from the bereaved family.

The *Methodist Times* article showed that the teacher : pupil ratio was still 1 : 7 as it had been in 1880, even though the Sunday School had more than quadrupled in the intervening half a century to 70 teachers and 500 scholars.

One of the scholars, who had entered the Sunday School in the Primary Department at the age of five and passed through each department, was Russell Stanley Morris. In a *Methodist Times article of November, 1933*, it was mentioned that Stan became assistant secretary of the School in 1917 and three years later was appointed General Secretary "of what is now the largest School in Reading. He is held in high esteem by the teaching staff for his quiet and efficient service to the cause of the children."

Later he was to become General Superintendent of the Sunday School and was remembered each year from 1984 by Sunday School members when they were presented with their Morris Awards. As the Superintendent of the Sunday School since 1984, I instituted those Awards that year in memory of both Stan and his wife, Ivy, who died within months of each other in 1982, having both given many years of faithful service to Whitley Hall Sunday School. The awards were presented for involvement in the life of the Sunday School, not just for attendance as had happened previously, so marks were awarded to those who attended extra rehearsals and took part in such activities as the annual anniversary and Toy services.

However, fifty years before those awards were first presented, at the Monday meeting following Sunday School Anniversary services the previous day, we read how, in 1934: "gratifying reports were presented by Mr Russell S Morris (General Sunday School Secretary), which showed a membership of 496 scholars and a staff of 57 teachers, the school being the largest in the town."

Seventy-two of those scholars of Whitley Hall Sunday School had received prizes for over 100 attendances and eighteen for 95 - 100 attendances from Mrs E J Mills the previous day. One scholar, Edie Howes, was the recipient of a gilt-edged hymn book for the maximum 104 attendances, being two attendances each Sunday throughout the year. Such loyalty had obviously been learnt from their teachers as, that same year, Methodist Sunday School Department Long Service Certificates were presented to:

Mr William John Hunter for 33 years service
Mr G J Cloke - 28 years service (15 years as superintendent)
Mr Albert Coppuck and Miss Ellen Cummins - both 27 years service
and Mr Arthur R Wells for 26 years service

Similarly, Miss E Swindon was presented with the 17th bar to her Juvenile Missionary medal, having collected £85 in 17 years. Eighteen others received JMS Certificates and Seals, raising a total of £62 *7s* *8d* during the previous year. We do not know when Whitley Hall Sunday School members first started to collect for the Juvenile Missionary Association, which started in 1903. In more recent years, it has been renamed the Junior Missionary Association nationally, and, at Whitley Hall, was under the leadership of Nigel Woodcraft, younger son of Joyce Woodcraft, who has already been mentioned in this chapter. However, it is obvious from the above that, by 1916, Whitley Hall's Sunday School was supporting that cause as it did until the Sunday School ceased when the Church transferred worship to the music room of the Avenue School on 16th November, 1997.

Mind you, 1934 was not the only occasion when Long Service Certificates were awarded to the staff of Whitley Hall's Youth Organisations. On Education Sunday, February 3rd, 1985, Rev John Stephens presented certificates for service to either Sunday School and/or Brigades, as follows:

53 years:	Sylvia Main *
52 years:	Reginald Sherwood *
43 years:	Leslie Bainton
42 years:	Leslie Norton
41 years:	Norman Rivers *
35 years:	David Allaway *

33 years:	Margaret Allaway * & Peggy Few *
30 years:	Phyllis Harris
25 years:	Daphne Barnes-Phillips, David Main*, Peter Sayers * & Stephen Sherwood *

In the case of those marked with an asterisk, their entire service had been at Whitley Hall. Of the grand total of 462 years, 375 of those were given to the youngsters of Reading through the work at Whitley Hall. A certificate should also have been presented to Edna Turner but she was sadly killed in a road accident on New Year's Day of that year. Her certificate for 50 years service was framed and hung in the Small Schoolroom in her memory.

Unfortunately, no photographs seem to have been taken on either of those occasions but, when a similar presentation was made on February 12th, 1995, the following were photographed with Rev Dr John Ogden who had made the presentation. They are (with their years of service) from the left:

Back row:
Rev John Ogden
Norman Rivers
(51 years),
Daphne Barnes-Phillips
(35 years)
Nigel Woodcraft
(25 years)
Front row:
Pamela Edmonds
(24 years)
Joan Eggleton
(27 years)
Phyllis Harris
(40 years).

The post Second World War Years in the Sunday School were described by Bernard Law who came to live in Whitley Street over a newly-opened pharmacy just three doors from Boots the Chemists in 1949. He wrote from Cheshire 40 years later and 25 years after leaving Reading for the *May/June 1989* (and also the *May/June 1986*) edition of *Newslink* as part of an article entitled:

"Sunday School was held both in the morning and afternoon. Two departments - one for the younger and one for the older age groups - met before the morning service. The latter, which, at times, numbered as many as 60 children, was led by Albie Coppuck (who, with his wife and daughter, Vera, took splendid care of the extensive premises). Vera also served as pianist then. At the same time, the Boys' Brigade Bible Class was held, led by Captain Reg Sherwood. The Children's Address was a helpfully interesting part of the morning service, which some of the adults sometimes said they enjoyed more than the sermon which was preached after the younger children had gone home.

"On Sunday afternoons, the School met in four different Departments: Beginners, Primary, Junior and Senior, all staffed by teachers who endeavoured to attend the Monday evening Preparation Class. The session was opened with a combined act of worship and then it split into the four sections each with its own Leader. Mrs Daphne Barnes-Phillips' mother, Rose Barnes, has left an indelible impression on my mind of one who, for so many years, gathered the little children every Sunday afternoon for Whitley Hall Sunday School, walking them from and back to their homes, after teaching in the Beginners' Department.

Rose Barnes in 1968 helping five to seven year old girls of the 1st Reading Girls' Brigade Explorer Company count the halfpennies they collected towards the purchase of a Guide Dog

One of the first hymns they must have learnt would be one that we also were taught at that age 'Jesus loves me, this I know'.

"An account of the Sunday School would be far from complete if we omitted the Sunday School Anniversaries. Those were outstanding days when all the children took some part in one of the three services. Their parents, relations and friends came to look and listen, after washing and dressing the children attractively, and filled the galleries of the Church upstairs as well as all the chairs downstairs.

"It was remarkable that when Christmas Day fell on a Sunday in the 1950s, morning and evening services were held at Whitley Hall as well as an open session of the afternoon Sunday School, whereas only morning services were held in most churches on December 25th, 1988 and January 1st, 1989. Are we now giving our Lord Jesus Christ the prior, pre-eminent place which is his by right?"

Bernard's recollection of Christmases at Whitley Hall reminded me of other traditions that were associated with that season, including Christmas Fayres, Advent wreaths, Toy Services, decorating the Church Christmas tree, singing carols in Whitley Street and Christchurch Court and Christmas parties, as well as pantomimes. Christmas parties were held by each department of the Sunday School, sometimes before Christmas, sometimes afterwards, but they always finished with a visit from Father Christmas bearing presents for the children. Other organisations associated with the Church also held parties at that time or joined with other groups and visited pantomimes produced by other Churches when Whitley Hall was not producing its own Pantomime. When we were sorting through items prior to the sale of Whitley Hall in 1997, we were reminded of some of those occasions as we came across Cinderella's carriage and the costumes worn during the pantomimes.

The Toy Services always included a nativity scene so that the children of the Sunday School and other Youth organisations associated with Whitley Hall could present toys, games, books etc to the Baby Jesus. Since the presents were then given to charities, such as the Chronicle Appeal, for distribution to those who would not be receiving many presents, they had to be held early in December. However, the candlelit Carol Service, which sometimes incorporated a Christingle service, was usually held closer to Christmas Day and the Christmas Day service itself was an opportunity for the children of the Church to share one of their presents with the whole Church as they showed them to the officiating Minister.

One very memorable Nativity scene produced by the Sunday School for their annual Toy Service happened in 1986 when 5 members of one family took part - baby Jesus was portrayed by Deborah Goddard with her eldest sister Sarah as Mary and brother Simon as Joseph. Her other sisters, Rebekah (behind Sarah) and Hannah (to Deborah's right), were angels. Also in the photograph is David Cadwallader (2nd from right in the back row) who was UMIST's captain when the University of Manchester Institute of Science and Technology reached the final of University Challenge in March, 2000. His brother, Peter, and twin sisters, Elizabeth and Rosemary, are also in the scene.

Chapter XIII: Mortlake

Will your anchor hold in the floods of death,
When the waters cold chill your latest breath?
On the rising tide you can never fail,
While your anchor holds within the veil.

Chorus: We have an anchor that keeps the soul
Steadfast and sure while the billows roll
Fastened to the rock that cannot move
Grounded firm and deep in the Saviour's love.

Verse 3 of no 689 in Hymns & Psalms
by Priscilla Owen (1829 - 99)

It was in the 1970s that the Spring Gardens area of Reading was demolished. In the *June 20th, 1967* edition of the *Evening Post,* we read:
"Compulsory purchase of houses in five Reading streets will enable the council to provide new homes for more than 1,700 people in the Whitley Street area - almost twice the number there at present."

Apart from Whitley Street itself, the roads affected were Spring Gardens, Spring Terrace, Mount Street and Waterloo Road. It was suggested that the reason for the demolition was either that the houses were considered unfit for habitation or that they had a bad effect on the amenities. The Deputy Borough Architect, Mr W E Payne, commented that the Council would be able to rehouse the people displaced from the area and had made allowance for that in its current housing programme. Altogether, the redevelopment area comprised thirteen and three-quarter acres and a total of 379 dwellings was proposed.

In the first phase, it was hoped to provide 142 dwellings for 557 people. When the order had first been made the previous year, the Council already owned 21 houses in the area and had since acquired another 78 out of the 150 or so homes concerned. Terms had also been agreed for a further 12 properties and there were only three objections outstanding at the hearing that day and none of those were represented.

By 1970, Reading Council's housing committee had decided what form the redevelopment of the area bounded by Whitley Street, Waldeck Street, Essex Street, Milman Road and Collis Street should take. The first phase covered three and a half acres running along Whitley Street and Southampton Street. All the old houses which once stood on that site had been demolished by then.

At one time it was planned to build council homes on this area, but the committee had dropped the idea because of the huge cost involved in acquiring the land - £35,000 an acre - due to the method of compulsory purchase in operation at the time. Instead, they were hoping to sell as much of that land for shops as the council's planning committee would allow.

The second phase covering seven and a half acres would be redeveloped for 'medium-rise' council homes, possibly in blocks of maisonettes, three or four storeys high. It was estimated that the first homes in the second phase would be ready in the financial year 1973-74 and the majority in the following year, making 170 or so council homes in phase 2. However, that depended on the area being declared a clearance area, giving the council the right to acquire properties, demolish approximately 40 in 1971-72 and more than 100 in 1972-73. About 60 of these homes had already been acquired by then and, at that stage the committee had agreed to extend the redevelopment area by including the sites of 87 - 95 Spring Gardens, 46 - 64 Milman Road and a triangular piece of land to the west of the site of phase two.

By 1972, the area was described as derelict and Reading Corporation had published proposals to close lengths of Spring Gardens, Mount Street, Waterloo Road and Alpha Street before the redevelopment of the area could go ahead.

Residents of roads to the west of the area had expressed concern at these closures because access to the properties which lay behind would be solely from Elgar Road to Waterloo Road or from Essex Street, Spring Gardens and Lynn Street. Because of this, in the *April 28th, 1972* edition of the *Reading Chronicle*, the Deputy Town Clerk, Mr C S McDonald, announced that a new service road would be constructed before the old roads were closed, although it might have a temporary surface for some time.

He also promised to keep a close eye on Lynn Street, which was a particularly narrow thoroughfare unsuitable for additional heavy traffic, and which could be temporarily closed to vehicles almost immediately if its use became dangerous. The article mentioned that the Katesgrove Housing Association were undertaking that phase of the Whitley Street redevelopment and the accommodation would be built around pedestrian areas.

By 1974, residents in the area had even more to contend with when the life of a family living in a flat above a shop in Whitley Street was filmed for a BBC documentary intended to show the everyday life of an ordinary British family.

The six-part serial entitled *'The Family'* featured the Wilkins family. As the relationships between Margaret and Terry, their four children and three spouses or friends were revealed, it became apparent why that particular family had been chosen. Christopher was not Terry's child; Marion and her boyfriend were living together under her parents' roof; Gary, his wife and toddler son were in another room; and Heather's boyfriend was half-caste.

As well as the intimate details within the flat, the series showed some of the surrounding area as each half-hour programme commenced with an 'over the rooftops' zoom in above Jelly's Stores, known to many later as 'The Chocolate Box' (shown in the photograph on page 16 as LONDIS). Tom's visits to the Wellington Arms were frequent and then, of course, his and Marion's on/off wedding plans finally resulted in Rev E Donald Mason being approached to conduct the wedding ceremony at Whitley Hall Methodist Church. That meant that Don's fatherly chat with the intending couple in the Minister's Vestry was filmed, as well as the marriage ceremony itself, so both the interior and the exterior of the church featured in the programme.

In 1999, twenty-five years after The Family was filmed, articles appeared in the National as well as the local press, giving updates on what had happened to individual members in the intervening years. In the *March 31st, 1999* edition of the *Daily Mail*, Lynda Lee-Potter, who had spent a day with the Family as a reporter 25 years before, reminded everyone of the real star of the show under the heading "Margaret, housewife superstar". This was followed a week later in the *Reading Standard* with Louisa Pritchard's update on all family members who appeared in the fly-on-the-wall documentary. At the end of the month an article entitled "The non-royal family that put Reading on the map and upset an MP" appeared in the *Chronicle.*

A decade after the filming, another part of Whitley Street was also preserved for posterity, although not in its original location. In 1985, when the central part of the Blake's Lock complex of buildings on the River Kennet was converted into a museum, the most attractive showpiece was considered to be the entire contents of the business that had operated at 3, Whitley Street from 1907 under the name of H Pottinger. In an article in the *October 11th, 1984* edition of the *Reading Standard* describing its proposed reconstruction in the Blake's Lock Museum, it was stated:

"H Pottinger's was a hairdresser of distinction, boasting marble topped basins with brass fittings over the mirrors. Original panelling survives along with the old signs, and the shop even comes with its shaving mugs and towels."

H L Gilbert Heath later described, in the *October 25th, 1984* edition of the same newspaper, his memories of Pottinger's Barber Shop:
"My father used to visit Mr Pottinger's establishment, I did, and then my two sons followed in due course, these visits to what is, by any standard, a remarkable shop. (There were two barber generations of the Pottinger family).

"There was no chromium plating, only the traditional polished copper of the water-heater. Marble-topped basins, barber's chairs with huge iron foot-rests and an array of chemist's sundries like moustache controller, hair restorers, brilliantines, Tatcho (what was that?) and a most impressive array of cut-throat razors.

"Customers sat against the dark panelling under coat hooks and there was room for a dozen all told. Normally the atmosphere was very thick with cigarette and tobacco smoke in my childhood days, and Mr Pottinger was not one to keep silent but engaged in spirited dialogue with all and sundry. On occasions, when politics was the subject, voices were raised and barbering operations temporarily suspended whilst the scissors and comb were frozen in mid-air, but it was all good natured, and, to visit Mr Pottinger was, in fact, a social occasion."

Chapter XIV: Digging new Channels

We expect a bright tomorrow,
All will be well
Faith can sing through days of sorrow,
All, all is well.
On our Father's love relying,
Jesus every need supplying,
Then in living or in dying
All must be well.

Verse 3 of no 525 in the Methodist Hymn Book
by Mary Peters (1813 - 56)

So what is the Spring Gardens district like at the start of the third Millennium? Many people think that the character of the area has changed considerably now that some of the narrow winding roads of terraced houses have been replaced with blocks of flats. Instead of the intimate chatting over the garden fence, the current much-wider ethnic mix of people are separated from each other in blocks of flats which can only be accessed by using an entry phone. Such a system is not unique to the Spring Gardens area but, nevertheless, seems to be the price we have to pay for modern living. Unfortunately, the larger properties in Milman Road and Basingstoke Road end of Whitley Street are today, in times of smaller families, more like the blocks of flats in that they are given over to multiple occupancy.

However, there are still pockets of original terraced housing, especially in Essex Street. In fact, in the January 18th, 2001 edition of the Chronicle, that area of Spring Gardens featured as a crazed driver of an Iveco truck had caused thousands of pounds worth of damage to the doors and mirrors of 21 vehicles parked in Essex Street as he reversed at high speed towards Whitley Street. Apparently, the lorry had initially hit a parked Fiesta near the end of the cul-de-sac at 9pm and when residents had appeared, he made a hasty exit!

The corner shops in the area have been superseded in this day of easier transportation by a concentration on one side of Whitley Street only, except for a florist, launderette, Digital Satellite Shop and a cycle shop interspersed with terraced housing between Whitley Hall and the Wellington Arms.

On the main shopping side, which still has some flats above, there are, in 2001: two charity shops, a newsagent, a post office, insurance consultants, a bakery, a fruiterers, a wine merchants, an opticians, a dry cleaners, a bank, a chemist and a security shop as there were ten years before. However, the main difference in the past ten years seems to have been the trend towards bigger units, with two or three original shop fronts being allocated to stores or restaurants, and more units connected with the preparation of complete meals. Whereas there were two general stores then, there are now four – Hussain's meat and grocery, Alldays, ANA Oriental Supermarket and Londis. In comparison with no restaurants then, there are now four – Italian, Indian, Tandouri and Chinese Fish. The take-away market seems similar to then in that there are still three take-aways – two Chinese and one pizza. New additions include: a licensed betting office, dental care, army surplus and a second-hand shop. However, there is no longer an estate agents, a jewellers, a video hire or a hardware store and the only Public House to survive in the area is the one on the other side of Whitley Street - the Wellington Arms.

Christchurch School and Whitley Hall buildings are still in existence on the sites where they have been since 1868 and 1906 respectively. In the *July 5th, 1985* edition of the *Reading Chronicle*, both were mentioned in the same article, along with the houses in Milman Road. This was because the school had shown its commitment to maintaining the children's interest in the area where it is situated by producing a quilt made with patterns based on local architecture. Apparently, the patchwork quilt had been part of a project on the environment in which 29 schools participated and whose work was displayed in the Reading Teachers' Centre in Cranbury Road. The quilt produced by the pupils of Christchurch CE School was described in the article as follows:

"The result is a colourful piece of material of about 1.6 square metres and featuring brickwork patterns from the houses opposite the school and the Whitley Hall Methodist Church at the end of the road." The headmistress, Mrs Gloria Isaacs, commented that it had taken four or five months to complete but was well worth the effort as the children had really enjoyed working on such an imaginative project.

The timing of the article and photograph was most fortuitous as far as Whitley Hall was concerned as it appeared in the week of the 80th anniversary of the stone-laying ceremony for that Church.

At the time of starting to write this section (August 6th, 1990), the school had featured in the *July 27th* edition of the *Chronicle* under the heading "*School's farewell to popular Teacher*" when Mrs Muriel Swann retired after teaching for 21 years at the school. Similarly, only the week before, the Chronicle had covered the life of someone whose memories have been quoted in this book - Mrs Sylvia Main - under the heading "*Death of a respected member of the Methodist Church.*"

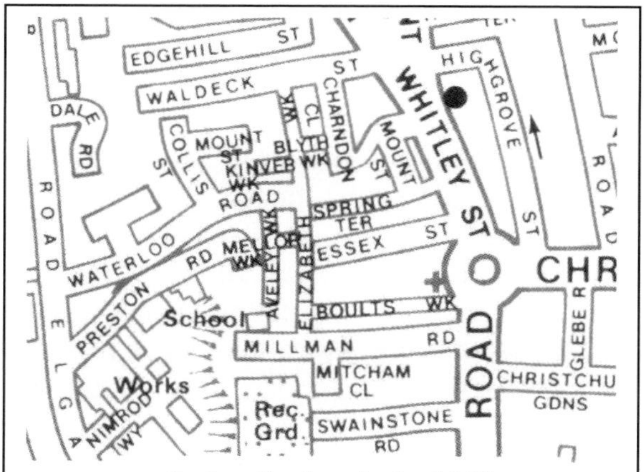

Spring Gardens in the 1990s

A look at the present layout of the Spring Gardens area reveals that, apart from Milman Road, Whitley Street, Essex Street, Waterloo Road and Christ Church School, the redeveloped area bears little resemblance to its 1899 design. After the example of Boult's Walk, Kinver, Elizabeth, Aveley, Blythe and Mellor Walks appeared in the 1970s when the area finally lost its core road, Spring Gardens.

Having considered the current layout of Spring Gardens, what does the future hold for that area of Reading? As well as losing its core road, it has become swallowed up in the Borough of Reading with very little remaining to give it a separate identity. Consequently, the pride that its inhabitants once felt in belonging to such an area is soon likely to be even more eroded as the older people move away or die. They will be replaced by those who naturally feel no allegiance to an area which, after all, has very little left to remind us of its past.

Agreed there is still the Spring Gardens Band, which plays each summer as part of a rota of local bands in the Forbury Gardens. However, it no longer practises in the area and it is probably not generally known how it came by its name. There is even an area to the south of Reading which is now called Spring Gardens so that could add to the confusion.

As well as the lack of identity within the area as a whole, the school, although still designated Christ Church C E School, ie an Anglican foundation, has for many years opened its doors to those children whose parents wish a Christian education, not specifically Anglican, for them. Consequently, several of those who attended Whitley Hall's Sunday School in the 1990s also attended that day school, so it could be said that the school's identity is now not as clearly defined as it was. On the other hand, others might applaud the Christian unity aspects which Christchurch School now manifests, rather than a strictly sectarian approach as previously.

In the 1990s, Whitley Hall Methodist Church attracted its members from a much wider area than just Spring Gardens and nearby streets as it tended to do in the days before the population became more mobile. Some of its members even drove past other Methodist Churches to worship at Whitley Hall where they felt that their needs were most suitably met. A survey of the membership undertaken as part of the Circuit Town Centre Neighbourhood Committee Project at the beginning of January, 1991, found that 30% of the 112 membership did still live within 600 yards of Whitley Hall and 60% lived to the south of it, so it was not surprising to find that more than two-thirds of the 41 membership that responded to a questionnaire did not see Whitley Hall as a Town Centre Church but as serving South Reading or Whitley or being a local or suburban Church. Using more natural boundaries, it was found that approximately two-thirds of the membership then lived between the boundary roads of Basingstoke Road, Elgar Road, London Road, Redlands Road, Shinfield Road and the M4.

Groups, such as Girls' and Boys' Brigades, Sunday School, Women's Own, and Men's Institute were, by the beginning of the 1990s, much smaller than previously in their respective histories at Whitley Hall. However, in the case of the Girls' Brigade, two girls had transferred from 2nd to 1st Reading when Wesley Methodist closed its company, considering it too small to be viable.

Such a large Church building and its ancillary premises, with consequent upkeep now that they are over 90 years old, resulted in talks as to the best way forward in the late 1980s. From September 1st, 1989 until March 31st, 1991, a Community Link Scheme was set up in conjunction with Reading Borough Council to make space at Whitley Hall widely available to residents in the Whitley and University areas of the town weekdays and evenings, Monday – Saturday, 9am to 10.30pm. This was the second such project "which successfully combines the forces of Reading Borough Council with other agencies in the town to create a network of spaces available at reasonable charges for community use" - for meetings, clubs, workshops, dance and music.

The first such scheme had been at Ridgeway School and the Whitley Hall Scheme came about after the Council had hired Whitley Hall's ancillary premises for an After School Club prior to and during the building of the log cabin at Waterloo Meadows from September 7th, 1987 until April 28th, 1989. The Children's Centre in Waterloo Meadows was officially opened on Saturday, April 22nd, 1989.

The Seventh Day Adventist Church was one of the bookings that resulted from the opening up of the premises for wider community use because they had hoped to establish a Church in the South of Reading which they recognised as being "a largely unchurched region of the town". Adult Education classes in 'Keep Fit for the Older Lady' and Dog Training classes also started to use the premises as did the Reading Concert Singers and the Pentecostal Church.

More recently, the Church found itself grouped with Oxford Road, West Reading and Wesley Methodist Churches as Town Centre Churches. They were all large Mission-style buildings built around the turn of the century and the Reading and Silchester Circuit decreed in 1992 that those four Churches were becoming increasingly expensive to maintain so a plan of rationalising them into two Methodist Church premises was developed.

Firstly, the Oxford Road Church was sold to the Church of God Worldwide Mission - its final Methodist services were held on November 24th, 1996 - and its members have moved in with the West Reading Church prior to the building of a completely new Church on the Battle Hospital site. The combined Church is now known as Emmanuel Church. The following year saw the start on alterations to the Wesley Church buildings in Queens Road.

1997 also proved a year of many changes to the Spring Gardens area as Peter Stagg, who had been the headteacher at Christchurch CE Primary for 10 years had left at the end of 1996 to take up a similar post in a larger school in Woodley. Jeffery Harborne, a foundation governor, after describing the interim arrangements with an acting headteacher and deputy head, wrote for the *March/April 1997 Newslink*:

"It is hoped to appoint a permanent headteacher to start from September 1997. There are currently 155 pupils, divided among six classes, but numbers have gone down slightly from last year. The school has received a unique invitation to send thirty children to visit the Sealife Centre in Birmingham. Rail tickets for the journey have been donated by Richard Branson's new Cross Country Rail Network.

"Residential trips are being planned during the summer to Osmington Bay leisure centre in Dorset and to Ufton Court in Berkshire. The PCC has made a donation on behalf of the Christ Church congregation towards the costs of these visits. The school will be coming to Christ Church at 11 am on March 26th for an Easter service. Members of the congregation are cordially invited to join us on this occasion."

The appearance, on Thursday, July 3rd, 1997 of a 'For Sale' board on the wall of Whitley Hall confirmed for many what Norman Rivers, a lifelong member, put into words for the *September/October 1997 Newslink* under the title *My trip to Town* or *A Sentimental Journey*:

"On the morning of Thursday, 3rd July, I passed Whitley Hall in our local bus at 10.15 am. Seeing a ladder against the wall and a van marked 'Advert Signs', my suspicions were aroused . . . .
Returning by same transport at 11.15 am, my suspicions were confirmed. There on the wall was a "For Sale" sign.
Not normally prone to sentimentality, my feelings did give vent . . .
I shed a tear and a lump arrived in the throat . . .

IT HAD HAPPENED . . .
Our Church with all its memories had got its demise.
I wondered how our forebears would react to the "death knell" of their beloved Whitley Hall.
TEMPUS EDAX RERUM – TIME THAT DESTROYS EVERYTHING."

On August 20th, Whitley Hall's Church Council met to consider the 11 sealed bids that had been made by the previous Friday and followed the estate agent's recommendation that, according to Charity Commission law, it accept the highest bid of £210,000. This meant that the premises were bought by the Reading Hindu community for conversion into a Temple. 5 of the bids had proposed continuation as a place of worship; 4 had been for residential development; and there had been a dancing school and a nursery school interested in purchasing the premises.

There had been much deliberation as to the way forward for Whitley Hall Methodist Church and, eventually, consensus was reached that the congregation should remain together for worship at 10.30 am in the Music Room at the Avenue School. As a result, a change of name to Whitley Methodist Church was effected after the Closing Services at 10.30 am and 3 pm on November 2nd, 1997. Since the school is in the Basingstoke Road, the Church now meets outside the Spring Gardens area for the first time in its history. It still maintains its links with Christ Church where it holds its Coffee Mornings and Bible Study groups on Fridays, Whitley Wives on Wednesdays and Church Councils and other occasional meetings. However, its Tuesday Lunches and Women's Own are now held at Tyndale Baptist Church.

1999 saw the return to the area of one of its hidden monuments. Although I had never seen the Whitley Pump, I had often heard reference made to it by those older than myself. Imagine my surprise, therefore, when I saw on May 13th that a replica of it had been placed on the roundabout opposite Whitley Hall. In the *May 14th, 1999* edition of the *Chronicle*, there was a photograph of Christchurch C of E Primary School pupils with Councillor Trish Thomas as she unveiled the replica of Reading's 19th century Whitley Pump. Trish is deputy Transport Committee chairman and the Pump was deemed to be an ideal centrepiece to round off two years of environmental improvements to the surrounding area, including widening pavements, planting trees, more on-street parking and reducing some feeder roads to one lane.

Although the original purpose of the Whitley Pump - that of providing water for horses and cattle traders after they had toiled up hill from town - is no longer needed, the central feature does enhance a roundabout which, for as long as I can remember, has always brightened up the Whitley Street area with its profusion of beautifully coloured flowers. It is to be hoped that the return of the Pump to the area will halt the tide of decay that was beginning to manifest itself and bring prosperity flowing back into Spring Gardens.

Certainly, on the first Good Friday of the third Millennium in the *April 21st, 2000 edition* of the *Chronicle*, the Spring Gardens area featured twice with articles of substantial size by Sarah-Jane Russell about both Christ Church School and the Whitley Street Hindu Temple. Although the latter had had their community grant application turned down, Reading Council's Community Action chairman, Cllr Malcolm Powers, explained that the reason for this was that their application was for growth whereas the grants were allocated for everyday running. However, he said that the council is working closely with the temple to put together a business plan and submission to the national Lottery to fund a development officer and administration assistant. He added: "We are also working with them to locate a community access point with several computers and internet access at the temple. We will continue to support the work of the Hindu temple and work with them to secure funding to renovate their premises." Certainly, by the time Reading Online Communities had been launched at the Civic Centre on December 18th, 2000, internet access had been effected at the temple and 14 other sites.

The Reading Hindu community had celebrated its first anniversary with a party for its own worshippers, Whitley residents and Reading Borough councillors on Saturday, July 31st, 1999. They currently offer meditation, yoga and language classes, daily coffee mornings, exercise for the elderly and disabled and youth groups – and, like the Methodists before them, these are open to all the community – not just Hindus.

For the second article, the title - *School celebrates a fresh start* - also suggests a more promising picture for Christ Church School than its recent history has shown. After running into trouble in 1998 when it failed an OFSTED

inspection, it has since gained the support of parents and the community who campaigned to save it from closure when councillors proposed that course of action to combat falling admissions. As a result, Christ Church CE Primary in Milman Road became the first English primary school to be involved in the government's fresh start initiative. This entailed closure then re-opening after the Easter 2000 holiday with new staff and a new name - New Christ Church CE (Voluntary Aided) Primary School. At the end of the Spring Term on Friday, April 14th, pupils lit candles to symbolise a new beginning for the school and acting head-teacher, Mrs Maggie Donaldson, described the importance of the ceremony for marking the new beginning and also the past:
"The school does have a very positive history and, although it has had bad times, it is now looking forward to a very bright future."

For the sceptics among you, Education chairman, Cllr Jo Lovelock, denied that the fresh start initiative is only a veneer:
"Not only do we have new staff and a new head but, with the support of the Diocese of Oxford in making the school voluntary aided, there is new investment in the buildings which will take place during the summer break. We are ensuring children there have access to teaching and other opportunities you would expect in a normal primary school which simply wasn't the case before we gave them a fresh start."

Another part of Spring Gardens whose future is in doubt at the beginning of 2001 is Pottinger's Barber Shop. Having received lottery funding to refurbish Reading Museum, the director of Reading museums, Karen Knight, told the Friends of Reading Museums that the council would not be able to get any more funding to renovate Blake's Lock and a commercial partnership was the only way forward for the site. This was reported in the *January 18th, 2001* edition of *Central* under the title *Canal museum being 'sold off'*, when supporters of Blake's Lock were told that the museum was to be leased for 999 years to a restaurant group. Former Mayor of Reading, Janet Bond, who helped to create some of the displays in Blake's Lock Museum, including Pottinger's Barber Shop, said that they "would be lost because the turbine room and screens room which would be retained as a museum after the restaurant conversion would not be big enough to house all the displays."

Over 30 years ago I recall that Reading Borough Council had a plan to widen the Basingstoke Road into a dual-carriageway to improve access to the town from the South. As a result anyone wishing to sell their property had to sell it to the Council. In 1974, therefore, this is what my father did to the house where I had spent the first 30 years of my life. As many of you will be aware, the house was never demolished for road-widening and is now likely to be standing for many years to come because, in 1999, the Basingstoke Road Relief Road was opened instead. That, and the "Park & Ride" scheme at the Madejski Stadium, has diverted much of the traffic heading into the town centre from the South and the M4 away from Spring Gardens. This takes my story almost full circle as the Spring Gardens area of Reading can now hopefully revert – at least partially - to its more tranquil origins, although I fear it is unlikely that the water and gardens will ever be seen again in their original profusion, now that the conduit has disappeared beneath the carpark at the top of Highgrove Street.

Another of Len Cook's sketches from memory of the original Whitley Pump, which stood at "The Top of Whitley"

Lay-Pastors & Ministers who served this "Society of the Methodist People"

Minister & dates	Main Events
Rev WT Kitching 1905 - 1907	Women's Own started - Oct 1905; Children's Sunday then week's Mission; Opening Ceremony of Whitley Hall and PSA formed 1906; Benevolent Fund & Management Committee 1907
Pastor A Fred Olsen 1907 - 1910	Inauguration of Boys' Life Brigade in 1909; Spring Gardens Wesleyan Band gave its first sacred concert in one of the public parks on Sunday afternoons 1909; aggressive Christian work for winter 1909-10; band marching round neighbourhood once a month Sunday evenings, calling attention to Hall services
Pastor TD Hicks 1910 - 1911	Notice board for advertisement of preachers; Temperance Society & Committee for Open Air work formed
Pastor Alfred Kemp 1911 - 1913	Great Bazaar was so successful that balance of outstanding loan was repaid by Easter 1913
Pastor Allen Stocking 1913 - 1920	Young Men's Institute formed after First World War; joint war memorial with Christ Church 1920
Pastor Bert Bailey 1920 - 1922	Fancy dress football match Boxing Day; annual Garden Show instituted; weekly prayer meeting Saturdays & weekly concerts in winter
Pastor Fred Thorpe 1922 - 1925	Pipe organ installed; Renovation Scheme undertaken & envelope scheme started 1923; Girls' Life Brigade 1925 after BLB restarted in 1924

Pastor E Carter 1925 - 1928	Membership 217 - 46 young people gave their hearts to God on March 20th, 1927
Pastor JW Spargo 1928 - 1936	Rev Morley Waite became a Missionary in 1929; formation of GLB Cadets & annual Church garden party 1933; membership of Sunday School reached over 500; gospel to Whitley housing estate residents
Pastor George A Dear 1936 – 1938	New set of rules for choir members
Rev JC Priestly 1938 - 1944	Restrictions during war years
Rev Wilfred M White 1944 – 1949	Living Statuary in November, 1948; annual Candlelit Carol Service introduced
Rev Bill Beddard Smith 1949 – 1954	Renovation in 1950; Student Campaign April 1954; Membership 258
Rev Gordon A Durrant 1954 - 1958	Wrote: "Prospect and Retrospect" about Whitley Hall; Rebuilding Scheme - birthday months groups
Rev Noel Richardson 1958 - 1963	Building of new kitchen and toilets; Whitley Forum 1962; Shilling-a-week Fund introduced 1960
Rev Edgar Richards 1963 - 1968	Newsletter 1963; introduction of Gift Day and Family Services 1964; House Fellowships 1966; visitation of Northumberland Avenue Estate by Christ Church Parish & ourselves, Edgar PhD 1967
Rev E Donald Mason 1968 - 1975	Roof renovation, Whitley Wives & Harmony Gospel Group, 1971; Don became Methodist Hospital Chaplain & President of Local Free Church Federal Council; Children's & Brigades' Corners (1973 - 74) dedicated in memory of Rose Barnes & Rose Upton

Rev Tony Daw 1975 - 1982	Michael Winch ordained, 1977
Rev John S Stephens 1982 - 1986	Superintendent Minister of newly-formed Reading & Silchester Circuit, started Circuit Office at Whitley Hall; *Newslink* started 1984 with Christ Church
Rev Alan F Elgar 1984 - 1990	Joint ministry with John Stephens at Whitley Hall & Wesley; Lay Assistants - Jo Burkey; Marion Cruddas; Link Scheme with Reading Borough Council for wider use of premises 1989-91, including facilities for disabled
Rev Jean Holyhead 1990 - 1992	First woman Minister at Whitley Hall in joint Ministry with Oxford Road Methodist Church
Rev Derek Shaw 1992 - 2001	Also joint with Oxford Road Methodist; move to the Avenue School as Whitley Methodist November 1997
Rev Dr John Ogden 1994 – 2001	Minister in Local Appointment who was also Head of Computer Studies at the University of Reading til his retirement; Lay Assistant: Margaret Locke-Wheaton

From left: Rev John Stephens with Rev Eric Essery welcoming Lord Donald Soper to Christ Church on the occasion of the celebration of the 250th anniversary of John Wesley's conversion on May 24th, 1988.

Sources

Anniversary Booklets

1927 *Souvenir of the 21st Anniversary of Whitley Hall, formerly Spring Gardens Mission*

1928 *Rainbow Bazaar Official Guide and Quotation Booklet*

1953 *Whitley Hall Methodist Church, Reading Year Book and Anniversary Report*

1954/5 *Whitley Hall Methodist Church, Reading Year Book and Anniversary Report*

1955/6 *Whitley Hall Methodist Church, Reading Year Book and Anniversary Report*

1956 Durrant Gordon A, *Retrospect and Prospect. The Story of Whitley Hall Methodist Church. Golden Jubilee1906 – 1956*

1958 *Whitley Hall Methodist Church, Reading 52nd Anniversary March 9th and 12th, 1958*

1966 *Whitley Hall Methodist Church Diamond Jubilee*

Auction Details

1849 April 5th, by Haslams under the will of John Boult

Berkshire Chronicle

1849 March 3rd, 24th, 31st; June 23rd and 30th; July 7th, 28th; August 18th; November 24th; December 1st

Books and Pamphlets

1895 Guilding, J M (Vicar of St. Laurence) *Notable Events in Reading*

1905 Childs, W M *Story of the Town of Reading*

1908 Clutterbuck, W S (Town Clerk) *Reading Corporation Terrier*

1910 Childs, W M *The Town of Reading During the Early Part of the Nineteenth Century*

1930 Tosland, W compiled by, *Tour Around Reading 1920 - 30*
1968 Luxton, G M (Head Mistress) *Christchurch C.E. Primary School Reading 1868 - 1968*
1973 Jordan, Mabel F ed by. *Wesley Methodist Church, Reading Centenary Souvenir Brochure 1873 - 1973*
1976 Yeo, Stephen *Religion and Voluntary Organisations in Crisis*
1977 Bates, Jim *The Methodist Church*
1980 Phillips, Daphne *The Story of Reading*
1988 Ayres, May *As Stupid as Oxen – A history of the Reading and Silchester Circuit*
1988 Moody, C R *Lovefeasts - Records and Memories of an old Methodist Custom*

Circuit Plans for the Wesleyan Methodist Church - Reading Circuit

1894 April 8th - July 1st
1895
1908 April - July
1914 - 1925 inclusive

Deeds - Conveyancing Papers, November 30th, 1904

1849 20th June, John Boult's land sold to Mr William Bishop; addendum: 30th November, 1904 when Sarah Kingham sold to Rev Owen Watkins, Thomas May & 18 others
1850 30th January, John Boult's land sold to Mr Wm J Pledge
1850 28th March, John Boult's land sold to Mr James Haslam
1864 26th August, Conveyance of Rose Cottage from William Thompson Pledge to Thomas Barkshire
1900 19th September, Conveyance of the Laurels, 6, Boult's Walk from Mrs Eunice Allport to Mr Wm S Allport

Evening Post

1967 20th June
1970 12th November

Hymn Books

1933	The Methodist Hymnbook
1950	The School Hymn Book of the Methodist Church
1983	Hymns and Psalms - A Methodist and Ecumenical Hymnbook

Maps

1840	Plan of the Parish of St. Giles, Reading, including the hamlet of Whitley in the County of Berks surveyed by W H Fuller, landsurveyor (Tithe Map).
1840	A New Plan of the Borough of Reading drawn & engraved by Edward Weller, pub John Snare Bookseller, 16 Minster St., Reading
1877	Surveyed by Capt G W, Archer, R E Levelled by Capt W Wynne
1899	Map of Whitley Hill in the Borough of Reading

Methodist Recorder

1974	June 27th	1991	June 13th
1985	February	1999	December

Methodist Times

(NB: Methodist Times and Leader merged with the Methodist Recorder in 1937)

1933	November
1934	January

Minutes Books

1892 - 1911	Minutes of Leaders' Meetings of Spring Gardens Mission
1907 - 1911	Minute Book of Whitley Hall Management Committee
1922 - 1933	Minutes of Whitley Hall Leaders' Meetings
1923 - 1953	Whitley Hall Women's Own Minute Book of Meetings
1924 - 1957	Minutes of the Whitley Hall Wesleyan Mission Choir
1930 - 1949	Minutes of Meetings held in connection with The Whitley Hall Wesley Guild
1977 - 1986	Minutes of meetings of Whitley Hall Choir

Newslink - joint magazine of Christ Church and Whitley Hall

1985	July/August edition			
1986	January/February,	March/April,	May/June	
1988	January/February,	March/April,	May/June,	July/August,
	September/October			
1989	January/February,	May/June,	July/August,	
	September/October,	November/December		
1992	January/February			
1995	July/August			
1997	March/April	September/October		

Personal Memories of:

	Dates	Page references
Albert Edward Barnes (Ted)	(1908 - 1988)	5, 91
Gladys Clifford	(1907 - 1997)	73-74,108
Robert Cooper (Bob)	(1922 -)	11,61,91-96,115-116,128-9
Charles A F Gibson	(1921 -)	32-33,54-55,67
H L Gilbert Heath	(1908 -)	53,66-67,140
Bernard Law (Tom)	(- 1991)	51,133-135
A E Keep	(1904 -)	126-127
Sylvia Main (nee Smith)	(- 1990)	45,52,98,101,132,143
Catherine Montague (nee Cox)	(1915 -)	60,101
Richard Painter (Dick)	(1905 - 1991)	68-9,91
Leonard Rapley (Len)	(1902 - 1996)	8,61,65,89-91,100,103-4 109-111,121-124
Norman Rivers	(1919 -)	132-3, 146
Robert Russell (Bob)	(1932 -)	55-57
Raymond Searle	(1915 -)	46,64,67,105,127
G E Watkins (Ted)	(1921 - 2000)	62-64
A Rosa Wilson (nee Agnes Dixon)	(1906 - 2000)	61,104,107,125-126
Elizabeth White (Liz)		118-120
Rev Michael Winch	(1936 -)	50-51,153

Their years of birth, where known, and death, where applicable, are shown in brackets.

Reading Chronicle

1972	April 28th	
1985	February 3rd	July 5th
1990	April 20th	July 20th & 27th
1999	May 14th	
2000	April 21st	
2001	January 18th	

Reading Chronicle Midweek

1986	April 15th	
1987	September 15th	
1989	November 22nd	
1995	July 26th	August 9th

Reading Mercury, Oxford Gazette, Newbury Herald & Berks County Paper

1833	October 14th & 21st	November 11th	December 28th
1842	December 3rd		
1854	August 26th		
1870	September 3rd		
1871	January 7th & 28th	September 9th	November 25th

Reading Observer

1912	May 4th

Reading Standard

1891	March 13th	June 5th	August 7th
1905	July 12th		
1906	March 17th		
1984	October 11th, 25th		
1985	April 25th		
1999	April 7th		

Roll of Honour

For First World War: 1914 - 1918
For Second World War: 1939 - 1945

Street Directories

1830 Pigot's Directory of Berkshire
1839 Yorke's Reading Street Key
1841 Fernyhough's Reading Directory
1842-3 Snare's Reading Directory
1847 Snare's Berkshire Post Office Directory
1853 Macaulay's Berkshire Directory
1856 Macauley's Berkshire Directory
1859 Macauley's Berkshire Directory
1860 Macauley's Reading Directory
1865 Macauley's Reading Directory
1870 Macauley's Reading Directory
1871 Macauley's Directory of Reading
1874 Webster's Reading Directory
1875 Smith's Reading Directory
1876 Smith's Reading Directory
1882 Smith's Reading Directory
1884 Smith's Reading Directory
1895 Smith's Directory of Reading
1902 Smith's Directory of Reading
1903 Smith's Directory of Reading
1906 Smith's Directory of Reading
1909 Kelly's Directory of Reading
1909 Smith's Directory of Reading

Year Books

1880 Year Book of Historical, Statistical and General Information for Reading